GRANDPA'S TIPS ON MANAGEMENT FOR ALL

COL (RETD) BHASKAR SARKAR V S M

ISBN 979-888503398-5

The book is dedicated to housewives and young men and women who go about managing their lives without understanding principles of management

Contents

Foreword

I have known Col Bhaskar Sarkar for over four decades and have always admired his prolific writings on various subjects.

"Grandpa's Tips On Management for All" is an insightful and informative recollection of real-life experiences that make a lasting difference and enhance our life.

The nuggets of information shared in this book cover a wide gambit of subjects and is interspaced with real-life examples from his life's journey in a very simple and forthright manner. **It is an ideal handbook that serves as a "management capsule for a layperson."**

You can make out that all the tips in the book come straight from his heart; which is the essence of his great observation and teaching abilities.

As brought out in the book, Grandpa has come across many people of all age groups who do not seem to know their purpose in life! If you wish to run through a maze of life confidently and arrive at the destination that you seek, this is the ideal book for you. It covers in detail, and very simple manner, how to achieve your targets and allocate resources to get the desired results.

There are anecdotes and real-life incidences that incorporate the essence of goal setting, behavioural psychology, motivation, risk assessment, planning, execution, transactional analysis, and developing leadership qualities. Besides this, there are also practical tips on issues like staying healthy, managing fear and surviving in an increasingly competitive and dangerous world.

"If life must have a goal, we must learn to set it."

This book is perfect for everyone who wishes to find a purpose in life and achieve lasting "peace and happiness."

I am profoundly honoured to invite you into making this book a part of your life, as you deserve the best!

Dr (Col) CP Ramchandani
Former Director SRM University
& Motivational Speaker
Chennai (India)

Preface

Grandpa believes that every person, whether a housewife, a school teacher, a student, a sportsperson and so on **is a manager**. Each person has to set targets or results to be achieved in many fields every day. They have to plan how to achieve their targets and allocate resources. They have to understand the basics of management to achieve their targets efficiently. **In this book, Grandpa tries to explain the basics of management to the layperson**. He also gives some tips on issues like staying healthy, managing fear and surviving in an increasingly competitive and dangerous world. Grandpa also tries a new concept of highlighting **key words**to help his readers to speed read the book.

Grandpa believes that we must all strive to be efficient. He believes that **an efficient person is one who achieves desired results consistently with minimum effort.**" The definition has two aspects. First key words are "**desired results**". The second key words are "**with minimum effort**".

Who decides what is the desired result?In an organization it is the "Boss". He is the one who lays down the targets or results to be achieved. There are two kinds of bosses. The first category are bosses who believe that targets set will not be achieved. They set unrealistic targets and are satisfied if 60% to 70% is achieved. The staff always fail to achieve targets and some are demotivated and give up giving their best and just go through the motions of trying. The second category of bosses set realistic targets. The staff usually achieve the targets. Everyone is satisfied. Everyone remains motivated.

At home, parents set targets for children. They can also be categorized like the bosses and set impossible targets. This sometimes results in some kids being unable to cope with expectations of parents and get into depression and some take to drugs, smoking or alcohol. A few of them even commit suicides. **Rest of us set our own targets and try to achieve them.**We may have a variety of targets to achieve at the same time. We set financial targets or budgets, weight loss targets, earning targets and so on. We must also understand the term **minimum effort and efficiency**. This has been explained in the book.

Grandpa is only giving tips on being an efficient manager. He **is not laying down any commandments or dogmas.**He is sure that his readers are intelligent enough to take what they find useful and reject the rest. He would not like to die without sharing with younger generations the lessons life has taught me.

This is my second book as Grandpa.The first, "Grandpa's Tips on Navigating Through Life" has also been published in partnership with Notion Press and available at Notion Press, Amazon and Flipkart.

The Author
October 2021
colbhaskarvsm@gmail.com

Acknowledgements

I am gratful to Sarita Sharma for designing the cover of this book

CHAPTER ONE

LIFE MUST HAVE A GOAL

We must have a goal in life. As children, some want to be like their father or mother. Others have other heroes they want to emulate. Some want to be cricketers. Some want to be soldiers. Some want to be actors or fashion designers. **Our goals keep changing as we grow up**. Goals may change when we recognize our talents or our abilities or get an opportunity and pursue them. Goals may have to be changed with changes in the financial condition of the family due to the demise of the earning member. Goals may have to be changed due to changes in physical state due to disease or accident. Goals may change due to war, natural calamities, changes in government policies of our nation or other nations like immigration and visa policies. Grandpa knows a young man who wanted to be a wrestler. He met with a motorcycle accident and lost his leg. He got a prosthetic leg and took up javelin throwing. He won a medal in the Para Olympic Games Tokyo 2021.

If we do not have a goal, we cannot identify the path that can lead us there. If we do not know our destination, we can be lost. We can go round and round in circles for a hundred miles without getting anywhere and remain where we started. Life must have a goal and a purpose. We must know what we want to be. **That can change with circumstances.**

There are two types of Goals. First is the **Ultimate Goal** and second are **Interim Goals**which lead up to the Ultimate Goal. His training in the army taught Grandpa to fix ultimate and interim goals. Ultimate goal is what we want to achieve at the end of our working life. A young officer joining the army may aspire to be a general. But before he can be a general, he has to do different courses, get good confidential reports and earn a number of promotions. These steps on the way to become a general are the interim goals.

We must understand ourselves and what we want and not be unduly influenced by parents and peers. One of Grandpa's nephews had done a degree in commerce, a degree in information technology and a diploma in management. He was contemplating doing masters in information technology. Grandpa asked him why he wanted to do it. He said because it is the in thing and his parents wanted him to do it. Grandpa asked him if he enjoyed writing programs. He said no. Grandpa asked him what he wanted? He said he wanted to get a good job. Grandpa told him to look for one. Soon he got a job to his liking and is well settled. His parents are happy.

Grandpa has a niece who was a brilliant student. She got a job with Tata Consultancy Services and became an expert in information technology. She was often sent abroad for assignments and was extremely well paid. But she could not cope with the stress created by her job and had a mental breakdown. She had to leave her job and be at home and undergo psychiatric treatment. She has recovered, re-joined information technology but takes up less taxing assignments. Maturing with age also helped.

Grandpa's son did badly in class X board examination and could not join the science stream. He joined commerce stream and after passing XII, did B Com and a two-year diploma in Computer Technology. After graduation he joined an IT firm in Chennai. The firm used to provide technical support to Citibank Chennai branch. Though without a degree in Computer Engineering, he was very good at his work. His company sent him to Citibank Singapore for a project. There the head of IT was so impressed with his work that he offered him a job at Citibank Singapore. The opportunity came. Grandpa's son took it. His goal of settling in India changed. He is now settled in Singapore.

Grandpa has come across many people, young and old, who do not seem to be very clear as to what they want out of life. Some are doing courses because their parents want them to be a doctor or engineer or an information technology professional. Some are doing courses because it seems to be the right thing to do or just because they are not sure as to what is the right thing to do. Very few are doing things they enjoy doing. **These persons need to focus on their strengths, weakness, opportunities and threats and set their goals in life.**

We cannot reach the goals of our life in one leap. We have to go through different steps or **interim goals.**If one wants to be a software engineer, one must pass class XII with mathematics. Passing Class XII with mathematics is an interim goal. Joining Indian Institute of Technology or some other renowned college could be the next interim goal. We have to work hard to achieve the interim goals which lead to our ultimate goals.

How does one go about setting goals?To set one's goal one has to determine what he or she wants to be and what he or she enjoys doing. To do that one must understand what is most important to him. This can be done by asking oneself some questions.

What do I really value?One can value money, power, social service, ideological cause or peace and harmony. Grandpa knows a kid in his neighbourhood whose sole aim in life was to make lots and lots of money. Grandpa has seen people give up lucrative careers to join politics or do social work or even become a priest. We read about suicide bombers and freedom fighters/terrorists who are ready to die for their cause.

Why do I value what I do?It is necessary to understand as to why one values what he does. Is it under the influence of parents, peer groups, advertisements or our own nature? If we do not understand this, what we think we value may be just a passing whim and we may regret the goal we set.

What is most important to me?To some it is money, to some it is power, to some it can be being able to enjoy what he is doing. To some, the career is most important. To some the family is most important. To a freedom fighter, the cause is most important. To get what is most important one must be prepared to sacrifice other things.

What is it that gives me the most pleasure?The answer to this question also helps us to understand whether the goal we have set is going to give us joy.

What do I most regret?The answer to this question gives you an understanding as to whether the goal you had set was appropriate and whether there is a need for change.

Once we know our destination, we must learn how to pursue what we value most. As a child and a young man Grandpa's interests were in sports, arts, literature, history and geography. But he realized that pursuit of these interests may leave him without adequate income to do things he wanted. He therefore followed his father's instructions and became an engineer. However, since he was not keen on engineering, he joined the Army. Grandpa had a very happy time in the Army. There were challenges, which he loved. There were plenty of juniors who could be helped to grow.

He had plenty of time to devote to his wife and children, to sleep in the afternoon, play games and pursue his hobbies. Grandpa never had much money or savings but he enjoyed life as best as he could, visiting places, driving around, dancing and partying. Then time came to hang up his boots, he needed money to remain happy and to fulfil his responsibilities. He joined the construction industry and became a civil engineer thirty years after he graduated.

Did Grandpa plan the path he followed? Not really. He knew what he wanted, "peace and happiness". He knew that to get it he had to have enough money to meet his needs and enough leisure to pursue his hobbies and to help people grow. He got a few lucky breaks, which enabled me to earn the money he needed. He took breaks, which enabled him to pursue his interests. He kept doors open for opportunities and took them when they came. Grandpa believes that is how it has to be. There are many roads to Rome. **There are many paths to our destination.**There are many crossroads on the paths. We must know what we want. We must pause at crossroads to decide what we do. A lot of pluck and a little luck will take us where we want to go.

If life must have a goal, we must learn to set it. What we want to be and what we want from life is one input. **The other is**an assessment of our strength, weakness, opportunities and threats. We should carry out **a SWOT analysis.**

First, let us look at our **strengths**. God has given some qualities and strengths to every person he has created. Some of us are handsome or beautiful. Some of us are very intelligent and good at studies. Some of us are good at games and sports and outdoor activities. Some are good speakers or orators and have a knack of convincing people. Some have talent for singing or acting. **We must understand our strengths and keep it in mind for setting our goals.**

Since we are human beings, we must also have our **weaknesses.**Some of us are not good looking. Some are poor at studies. Others are weak in the body or physically handicapped. **In setting our goals, we must keep in mind our weaknesses.**If you are weak in mathematics, you should not look for a career in science or engineering. If you cannot dissect a frog, you cannot be a doctor or a nurse. If you are not good at communicating and sensitive, you should not try for a career in sales. **We must also try to overcome our weaknesses.**

Life is full of **opportunities**but they are not available to all of us. Some parents have lots of money to educate their children, some parents are not so lucky. Some stay in cities with good education opportunities. Others live in rural areas where opportunities for higher education are non-existent. **We must learn to leave doors open to allow opportunities to walk in**.

Life is also full of **threats.** Lack or shortage of money is perhaps the biggest threat. Inability to compete is another. We must guard against these threats when we set our goals.

The analysis of strengths, weaknesses, opportunities and threats should lead us not only to set goals, but also to **prepare action plans to achieve them.**

Ultimate and interim goals can and will change with the progress made in battles and changes in the circumstances of life. Some of the reasons for changing interim and final goals may be the following:

Change in Physical Condition. Grandpa knows a young man who was keen on a career in the army. He met with an accident and became paralyzed below the waist. He had to change his goals. Some develop heart problems and have to look for less stressful occupations.

Change in Financial Conditions. Grandpa knows a young man whose father was working with a multinational company. His father gave up his job, started his own business and lost all his money. They boy obviously had to go in for a career where the cost of education was affordable.

Change in Mental Attitude or frustration. Mr. Ajit Jogi, Ex Chief Minister of Chhattisgarh gave up a career in the Indian Administrative Services to join politics. Mr. Bunker Roy gave up a career in the Indian Administrative Services to start an NGO.

Inability to Compete. Grandpa knows a boy who wanted to do business management. He could not pass the entrance examination. He changed to mass communication and is happy as an assistant director making television serials.

Inability to Achieve Interim Goal. Grandpa knows many friends in the Army who failed to get promotion to the rank of Colonel or Brigadier and left the Army to join the industry. He had to change his goal from becoming a general to becoming a successful company executive.

Grandpa did civil engineering. But his heart was not in engineering. He loved games and sports and an outdoor life. He joined the army. And even though he did not become a general, he enjoyed his 28 years in the army. He thinks he has achieved his goals in life.

For those who are young and have yet to set their goals, Grandpa recommends that you try to identify what you want to be and what you enjoy doing, identify your strengths and weaknesses and the opportunities and threats. Based on these inputs, set your ultimate and interim goals. Then work wholeheartedly to achieve it. **If you are in middle life and not happy or satisfied with what you are and what you are doing, take the same inputs and reset your goals. Once that is done work to achieve them. May God be with you.**

CHAPTER TWO

MANAGING LIFE

We go through life without realising that each one of us are acting as managers. The reality is that **we are acting as managers all the time**. Managing is getting things done or getting others to do things so that you get what you want. When you do something by yourself like shaving, bathing or driving you are not acting as a manager. When another person, husband, wife, children, maid etc is involved, you become a manager.

To manage life smoothly, we mustunderstand how things are done and **learn the basics of management.**The fundamental relationship between output, process and input is diagrammatically represented below.

OUTPUT <------------ PROCESS <------- INPUTS

The **output**is the end result we want. It can be the design of a house, a chicken dish or passing examinations.

Processis the method we adopt to get the output we desire. Let us say that the output we want is a new dress. We can adopt different processes to get the output. We can buy a ready-made one on line, go to a shop and select and buy; we can go to a tailor and get one stitched or stitch it ourselves.

Inputscan be classified into five categories; men, material, money, machines and time. All may not be needed for the output.

For managing men, we have **man management**or personal management or human resource management. At the domestic level it involves communicating, motivating or getting others to do what you want them to do. It is also the skill to make others like children and domestic staff give their best.

For managing materials, we have **material management**. Material management involves inventory management, purchasing, storing etc. At a domestic level it involves calculating what you need to run the house, having a policy on buffer stocks, purchasing and storing what has been bought. Considerable thought needs to go into this or you may find that you do not have what you need or perishables go bad and food stuff is not used by the due date. If storage is not proper, perishables will perish and rats and other pests or humidity will spoil what you have bought.

For managing money, you need **financial management**. When there is no shortage of money, this is not an issue. But where money is short, we need to understand the concepts of cash flow planning, opportunity cost and prioritization of expenditure. We must understand that money is essential to get things done. One must understand the importance of money and not over-spend or waste it on things we do not need. **"Shop till you drop" is a very bad idea. Spending money to show off is also a very bad idea.**

For managing machines, **we have to understand the concepts of preventive and break down maintenance, maintenance contracts, warranty etc.**

Managing timeis most critical. Time that is gone never comes back. Managing time is most difficult. Good managers understand how to do things simultaneously by good planning and **create spare time to think**or relax and enjoy. One example is cooking on two or three stoves at the same time or using gadgets like rice cooker or air frier. One must manage time so that **you have enough spare time to forecast, plan and do problem solving**.

Everyone in the house is a **manager**. Everyone must understand the functions of a manager.

The first function of a manager is **forecasting**. Forecasting is looking into the future and seeing what has to be done and when. A working person has to be aware of what is going to happen at the workplace like meetings, targets, tours, possible strikes etc. The housewife has to plan meals, shopping, entertaining etc. Anticipating likely price rises and shortages due to storm warnings, strikes and global trends will enable the housewife to stock up for difficult days. Children have to be aware of dates of examinations, annual days, tuition schedules etc. We have to remember birthdays and anniversaries etc.

The next task of a manager is **planning**for the events which are forecast. Let us take the example of a birthday function. We have to decide where it is to be held, who all are to be invited, what will be on the menu, what will be bought and what will be cooked, when is the cake to be ordered and by whom? One will have to decide on the dress, entertainment, presents and so on.

The next function of a manager is **directing.** The manager has to brief all those who are involved in organizing the function or doing a task and allot tasks and time by which they are to be completed. He also has to allot resources like money, time, transport etc. to those tasked.

The next function of a manager is **monitoring and controlling.** A manager has to supervise the execution of the task and see that things are progressing as planned. Quite often there will be problems. These will have to be sorted out or the task will not be achieved or the aim will not be fulfilled. **Please remember that you can delegate authority or work; you can never delegate responsibility.**

Please spend some time and effort in understanding the management process and functions and try to be an effective manager. It will go a long way in making life fruitful and enjoyable.

CHAPTER THREE

PLANNING IS THE KEY TO PERFORMANCE

Planning is the key to performance. Without proper planning we will not be able to do any task properly and efficiently or meet deadlines and live from crisis to crisis. It is therefore necessary to understand the planning process.

Planning is for achieving a particular goal or objective or task. For example, let us say that the objective is to get admission into a good college after class XII to get a degree in B Com.

The first step is to**review the information available and collect information.**Information is required for planning. Inthis example, information is required about the reputed colleges; method of admission e.g., entrance examination or class XII grades, fee structure, availability of hostel facility etc. Information not available must be collected before planning can commence.

The next step is to prepare an **action plan**. The action plan has to cover the various stages. In our example, the action plan could cover short listing the colleges you want to apply to; obtaining and submitting application forms. If the entrance examination is there, obtain details of past papers and start preparations. For highly competitive examinations like MBA, one may want to join a coaching class. If you are selected by more than one college, which one to join and why.

If the objective is a more complex one like construction of a house, the stages will be different. These could be to first select an architect and prepare detailed project reports and tender documents. Next will be the issue of tenders. Next you have to evaluate tenders and select a construction agency. After that you have to place a work order; prepare cash flow requirements and arrange resources. You will have to make arrangements for supervision and monitoring progress.

You will have to nominate a supervisor responsible for each task. Someone has to be in charge. Resources in terms of men, materials, machines, money and time have to be allotted. Assessment of resources required has to be realistic. Men must have requisite skills. Time required for tasks has to be realistic. Preparation of the work program by PERT/ CPM/Bar chart is necessary. Establish landmarks for monitoring progress. CPM even in rough form is best as it establishes slacks and interdependencies.

Once a plan is made, we must make **contingency plans.** Very few jobs get executed exactly as planned. As per Parkinson's Rule, if a thing can go wrong, it probably will. Therefore, once a plan has been made it is worth examining what can go wrong and plan as to what is to be done if something does go wrong. This is called contingency planning.

Each individual must **plan his week and day**. It is essential to list out tasks for the day. It is desirable to maintain a running list on which we score out tasks, which are finished and add new ones. The list can be on the computer. The list should include both personal and official matters and also instructions to be issued.

There will be a number of things to be done every day. Hence it is important to decide which should be done first. Issue instructions and distribute work before you start your own work. Do not keep your subordinates waiting or the work given to them will be delayed.

Keep deadlines, time for meetings in mind while deciding priorities. Deadlines must be met. If it is not possible to keep deadlines, the authorities or client must be informed in time so that they can take appropriate action. Creative work should be done when your mind is fresh and not under stress

Time Planning is most important. You must be able to assess time required for different activities. It is useful to record time taken for activities. The **critical path method**is a very good tool to assess time required for completing tasks or projects. Another method is preparing a **bar-chart**. These are not too difficult to learn. Any book on project management will have them. Now a days you can look them up in the internet.

One must remember Pareto's Law of the Vital Few and the Trivial Many. The law states 10% of our possessions are worth 90% of the value. 10% of what we do brings 90% returns. So please identify the vital few activities and concentrate on them. Delegate the trivial many to your subordinates and save time.

Detailed plans should be made for **visits and meetings**. One must prepare for a visit or meeting to derive maximum benefit from it. You may list out the following:

- What is the aim of the visit or meeting?
- What information do I have to collect?
- What documents and tools do I have to carry?
- What appointments do I have to fix?
- What is the time plan including time required for travel?
- What administrative arrangement including bookings, meals, equipment like slide projectors, cameras etc. and how much money should I carry?

Please remember that detailed planning is the key to successfully achieving your objective and avoiding crisis. To plan one must have time to think.

CHAPTER FOUR

EFFICIENCY

The **Output**is the end result we want. It can be the design of a house, chicken dish or passing examinations.

Processis the method we adopt to get the output. Let us say that the output we want is a new dress. We can adopt different processes to get the output. We can buy a ready-made one at a shop; we can go to a tailor and get one stitched or stitch it yourself.

Inputscan be classified into five categories; **men, material, money, machines and time.**

To start with we decide what is the output that we want? Then we decide on a process and provide the inputs. Let us take a few examples.

Output	Process	Inputs
Design of a house	Architect Firm	Information about our requirements. Information about site/plot Time by which required Fee and payment schedule
Chicken dish	Recipe	Chicken & ingredients Cook Gadgets like Tandoor, mixer grinder etc. Time Money to purchase
New Dress	Tailor's Services	Design Cloth and accessories Time Money

We are responsible for providing the inputs. If the inputs are not available, even the best process cannot produce the desired output.

Overall efficiency = Output / Input = Fee / Cost. The man hours required for a particular job depends of the following:

Knowledge / skill of a person. An expert designer will do a design faster than a junior design engineer.

Clarity of briefing. If the task is not properly understood, the chances are that the work would have to be done more than once. This is inefficient and adds to cost.

Quality of Equipment. Better the equipment, less will be the time taken to get the output.

If We want efficiency in operation, we must learn to look beyond cost to cost / benefit. Cheapest or the most expensive is not always the best solution.

A proper briefing to the person doing a task is most vital. If the task or output required is not understood, the task will have to be done more than once. Extra time spent in detailed briefing is never wasted. If the management is not clear about the output it wants, it can never get it. **It is always necessary to check back if instructions have been understood.Communication is not what has been said but what has been understood.**

We must be clear about the output we seek. For example, if a 5 kg washing machine meets our requirement, we should not buy a 7.5 kg one. When we want to buy a computer, we must know who is going to use it and what its configuration should be.

We must be **willing to provide resources**for what we want. Those tasked are not magicians. They can only produce results if required resources are provided.

We must understand**the concept of matching or coordinating resources.** This is particularly so when we employ a tradesman like a carpenter or painter to do something but have not procured materials for the task. Such unseen wastes add to cost and lower efficiency.

We must also understand the difference between **a perfect solution versus a workable solution.**Perfection requires a lot of effort which means a lot of time and perhaps money. Since resources, particularly time is limited, **seeking perfection in one activity often results in neglect of other activities**like spending time with family, taking physical exercise, sharing household chores and spending time on forecasting and planning. Seeking a perfect solution can sometimes lead to inability to meet deadlines. Finding a perfect life partner is almost impossible.

Another ability which makes us efficient is understanding the difference between **doing the right thing**and **doing a thing right**. The concept is best illustrated in the example where the lady of the house has invited a couple and cooked a delicious non vegetarian meal with kababs and biriyani. Unfortunately, the invited couple turned out to be vegetarians and food had to be ordered for outside.

We must also understand the difference between being **activity oriented**and **result oriented**. Most government actions are activity oriented. Government statistics will show how many trees were planted but never how many survived. Activity which does not produce desired results is a waste of resources.

CHAPTER FIVE

LEADER VS MANAGER

Leaderis one of the most difficult terms to define. Instinctively we can easily identify a leader in a group. He **is one who we expect will show us the way, who will tell us what to do to achieve our collective goal or to guide us in times of crisis. He is a person whom we admire and trust.**

A leader is always mentioned in relation to a particular group. We have **religious leaders**like Jesus Christ, Gautam Buddha or Guru Nanak. We have **military leaders**like Rommel, Patton or Netaji Subhash Chandra Bose. We have **political leaders**like Hitler, Churchill or Mao Ze Dong. We have leaders in the worlds of sports or fashion, **men and women who set the trends**for others to follow. We have leaders in our family, in our clubs and in our class.

What makes a leader?Why do we accept a person as a leader? What makes him tick? These are some of the questions which we will try to examine in this chapter.

Every human group activity needs the guiding hand of a leaderto direct the activities of the group and channel the energies of the group in achieving its goals. In the march of civilization, the first leaders were the leaders of tribes. They were usually elected. Then came the kings who inherited their kingdoms or created their kingdoms by defeating others. We have elected leaders like presidents or prime ministers leading countries with democracies. We have generals leading armies on the battlefields. We had religious leaders spreading different faiths. There are captains of industries who have established successful businesses. We have team captains and coaches of teams of games and sports.

The leader may be elected or nominated or hereditary. But they all have one mission. **The mission of a leader is to use the resources of the group to achieve the goals of the group.**

All leaders are not equally successful. India has seen thousands of kings and emperors but the names of Babar, Akbar, Rana Pratap or Shivaji find a special place in history. There were hundreds of generals who led armies in the Second World War. But Rommel, McArthur and Patton find special mention for their ability to inspire their troops to heroic deeds. Leaders are not always successful in their mission. General Montgomery won the battle of El Alamein but it is Rommel who was more admired and revered by the troops. Akbar's general and Maharaja Man Singh of Amber won many more battles than Rana Pratap, but it is Rana Pratap who inspires valour and admiration of the Indian nation. Very few remember Man Singh.

To be successful leaders we need to understand leadership.

Let us first try to understand the difference between a leader and a manager. A leader leads a group or team to achieve certain goals. So does a manager. Both work with people and other resources. But there are differences.

Leader	Manager
A leader can be elected, selected, appointed or hereditary.	A manager is appointed by the management.
A leader represents the interest of the group.	A manager represents the interest of the management or employer.
A leader sets the goals for the group.	The management sets the goals for the group and conveys it through the manager.
A leader works for the benefit of the group.	A manager works for the benefit of his employer and himself (profit, promotion, bonus etc.)
When a leader succeeds, the group always benefits.	When a manager is successful, the management always benefits. The group and the manager may or may not benefit.
A leader mostly leads from the front. He shares the hardships of his group. Alexander's pouring water given to him on the desert sand in front of his thirsty army is an example.	A manager mostly leads from the sanctuary of his office and rarely shares the hardship or dangers faced by the group.
Leadership is successful in the long run.	Management is successful in the short term

A leader has to be a managerto be able to achieve the objectives of his group. **A manager is rarely a leader**. A leader is people oriented. A manager is profit oriented. However, if a manager wants to be successful in the long run, he must imbibe the art of leadership.

"A" stands for abilities of a leader.A leader has to set and achieve goals for the group he leads. To be able to do that he needs certain abilities like mental alertness to be able to set popular and beneficial objectives. He must have the ability to plan, execute the plan and achieve the objective. He must be able to provide the professional knowledge required to execute the plan. He must be able to maintain harmony within the group and between the group and the environment.

"B" stands for the behaviour of a leader.A leader leads from the front. He dominates his group. He is visible to his followers. He constantly communicates with his followers telling them what to do and how to do things to achieve the group objective. He is always where the danger is and the action is. Leaders set examples for their followers.

"C" stands for the characteristics of a leader. These are traits which leaders should have and which make them successful. These are qualities like justice and fair play, courage, integrity, loyalty, patriotism etc.

"D" stands for dynamism of a leader.A leader has to be dynamic. He has to act all the time. He has to be able to maintain his hold on the group. He must be sensitive to the needs, hopes and aspirations of his group and of the individuals who make up the group. He must constantly monitor the mood of the group and the environment and act whenever necessary.

Every human group activity needs the guiding hand of a leaderto direct the activities of the group and to channel the energies of the group to achieve the aim. The leader may be elected or nominated or hereditary. All leaders are not equally successful. To be successful, as potential leaders we need to understand leadership. There are **three pillars of leadership**. These are selflessness, knowledge and character.

Selflessness is an essential requirement of Leadership.A leader has to identify himself with the needs, hopes and aspirations of the people. Mahatma Gandhi or Subhash Chandra Bose did not lead the freedom struggle or the Azad Hind Fauj for personal gains. They were ready to suffer mental and physical dangers and hardship to achieve their goals.

A leader needs two types of knowledge. **Professional knowledge**which would enable the leader to achieve the goal and **knowledge of human**

naturewhich enables the leader to motivate the group to give their all to achieve the goal.

Leaders must have **impeccable character**to gain respect or reverence of their followers.

Leadership traitsare the qualities of a successful leader. It is said that a successful leader has three basic qualities. These are selflessness, knowledge and character. I will try to explain these qualities.

Selflessnessis the foundation of leadership. It comes from total faith in an ideal or a cause. Selflessness is most difficult to acquire. It is imbibed during childhood through the influence of the mother who is mostly seen as being the most selfless person in the family. It is imbibed through the customs and traditions of sharing and caring in the family and society and by witnessing the examples of selflessness in leaders and personalities who are accepted as role models during our childhood and adolescence. It is faith or belief in the cause that enables men and women to rise above self-interest and self-preservation and give everything in quest of the cause or goal. The Rani of Jhansi could have lived and ruled if she had not defied the British Raj in search for independence. **Selflessness is the fountainhead of all virtues contained in a leader. It is also what differentiates a Leader from a Manager.**

A successful leader has to retain the faith and admiration of his followers. He has to work with the help of his group to achieve the goal. The Leader must know how to handle people. This knowledge of **man management** has three parts.

Human Psychology. A leader must know human psychology. He must understand how to arouse human emotions of anger and indignation at his enemies. He must understand how to keep the group committed to the cause. He must know how to keep the group faithful and loyal to his leadership.

Communications.A leader is usually a good orator. He must have good communication skills. He must be able to sell dreams. He must be able to indoctrinate members of his group to accept the justness and legitimacy of the cause, the goals and his leadership.

Theory of Motivation.A leader must know how to motivate members of his group to do his bidding without any fear or remorse about the consequences. Motivating a suicide bomber is perhaps the ultimate test of the motivational skill of the leader.

A leader has to achieve some objectives for his group. To achieve objectives, he must use resources available to him. **He must know how to prepare a plan to achieve his goal**.

A leader must know how to organize his resources to achieve his aim. He must know how to create and finance organizations. He must know how to create a hierarchy without creating conflict within the organization. He has to lay down a chain of command and succession. He has to develop systems for communications and security.

A leader may not have acquired his knowledge at a management school or at a formal school.A lot of this knowledge may have been acquired during discourses with wise men of their times. Many things might have been learnt intuitively during childhood and while growing up through exceptional powers of observation and reasoning. Aspiring leaders may have read or heard stories about the exploits of leaders they admired. They may have grown as an apprentice or lieutenant to some leader of their time and imbibed the knowledge. Modern leaders can pick up a lot of knowledge from the management schools and books and even from the internet.

Character has been defined as the sum total of an individual's personality. The character of a leader will generally be studded with the qualities listed below. Napoleon is reported to have listed 90 qualities.

A leader must at all times be **guided by the principles of natural justice and fair play**. He cannot be seen to favour any individual or sub group within the group. If he does so, the group will disintegrate.

A leader must have courage. Courage is of two types, **physical courage and moral courage**. Physical courage is the ability to overcome fear of death or physical injury and carry out one's duties. This is common at times of war or internal strife or natural disasters. A leader leads from the front and is seen where the danger is. Moral courage pertains to willing to stand up for what is right in the face of persecution or harassment or even death.

Integrityimplies honesty in financial dealings. It also implies willingness to honour commitments made even when doing so can cause financial loss or inconvenience. There cannot be trust between the leader and the follower if the leader lacks integrity.

A leader must be **loyal**to his group. **He must never criticize his group or its members in front of outsiders.**He must do his best to protect their rights and interests.

A leader must be **patriotic**. He must love and respect his country.

Initiativeis the willingness and ability to grasp fleeting opportunities and to act boldly to achieve the goal. A leader must have this ability.

A leader must be **capable of taking quick decisions and acting**. He cannot dither or allow things to drift.

A leader must have the **determination**to strive to achieve the goal in face of all adversity. He must not be deterred by failure or difficulties. He must be willing to keep trying till he succeeds or perishes trying.

A leader must be **mature**. He must not be upset by disagreement or dissent. He must not be excessively elated by success or demoralized by failure. He must be cool and calm and act according to the needs of the situation.

We may not possess all the attributes or traits of a good leader. But we can study our weaknesses and strengths through introspection and consultations with our friends and confidants. Once we have done that, **we can always improve.**There is no dearth of information or schools of learning. All that we require is the desire and determination to improve ourselves.

CHAPTER SIX

COMMUNICATION AND TRANSACTIONAL ANALYSIS

Effective communication is essential for success in our endeavours and living a conflict free peaceful life. This vital subject is rarely studied.

Communication is conveying our needs, feelings, requirements, appreciation, disapproval, instructions etc to others. **Communication can be verbal or non- verbal.**We all understand verbal communication. Analysis of verbal communication is called Transactional Analysis. Grandpa recommends that each one of you read the book "**I am OK: You are OK**"and try to improve our communication skills. This chapter hopes to encourage you to study "Transactional Analysis" and understand non-verbal communication and practice what you learn.

We have elements (**Ego states**as per management jargon) of **"Parent", "Adult" and "Child"**in our personality. **"Parent"**can be of two types. **"Critical Parents"**are always finding faults and want unquestioned obedience from the child and are ever ready to discipline the child for perceived wrong doing. They love to advise others. **"Nurturing Parents"**are loving and helpful. They will be agreeable and supportive. **"Adult"**is all logic and no sentiments. He wants others to behave rationally and sensibly. He gets upset with being told what to do, cannot tolerate illogical or impulsive behaviour and is upset by what he considers unfair criticism. The **"Child"**is impulsive, fun loving, imaginative and impulsive. He or she is always testing the limits of freedom, what activities he can get away with without parental rebuke or punishment. Children can be of two types; **obedient**or **rebellious.** When we speak, it is one of our three selves who speaks. If the wife says at 11 PM at night, "Let us go and have some ice cream", it is the child in her that is speaking. Usually, one of the three elements dominate our personality.

Transactionsare spoken exchanges between two persons which consist of a minimum of one sentence and its reply. For example:

A – "How are You?" B – "Fine, thank you."

Analysis of "Transactions' 'enables us to identify the operating ego state; understand personalities of those involved in the "Transaction" and understand the genesis of interpersonal conflicts. Transactions are of three types; Complimentary, Crossed or Ulterior.

Complementary Transactionsare messages sent and received from the same or complimentary ego states. They can be between adults and adults; parents and child; parent to parent and child to child. Complementary Transactions do not create conflicts. However, a message from a Critical Parent to a rebellious child will not be complementary and can lead to unpleasantness. Some examples of Complementary Transactions are given below:

Adult and Adult

Maid to mistress – "I have a problem at home. Can I have five days leave".

Mistress to maid – "Most certainly. Nothing serious I hope." Or; "I am having some guests next week. Can you manage for three days?"

Child and Parent

Wife to Husband while window shopping in a Mall – "What a lovely saree. Can I buy it?"

Husband (Nurturing Parent) – "I agree it is beautiful. Let us see whether we can afford it."

Husband (Critical Parent) – "You will never learn to control yourself. You think I am a millionaire? You already have so many. (This is not a complimentary transaction and could lead to conflict.)

Crossed Transactionsare transactions that are between ego states that are not complementary i.e., when the transaction originates in one ego state but the reply is given from another ego state. Some examples are:

Maid to mistress – "I have a problem at home. Can I have five days leave".

Mistress to maid – "You are only interested in taking leave and not doing work. No way. If I have to do all the work, why am I paying you?"

Wife to Husband while window shopping in a Mall (child to parent) – "What a lovely saree. Can I buy it?"

Husband to wife (adult to adult) – "Sorry. No money."

Crossed Transactions always hurt. They can lead to conflict if the recipient retorts back. E.g.

Wife to husband (rebellious child to parent) – "You have money to buy a saree for your sister but not for me."

Transactions between critical parent or adult and rebellious child will invariably lead to conflict. If one can sense the ego state from which a transaction is initiated and select an appropriate ego state to reply from, the conflict can be avoided and oil poured on troubled waters. E.g.

Husband (nurturing parent) to wife (rebellious child) – "I am sorry. I did not realize that you wanted it so badly. We will buy the saree. But let us first have an ice cream." The fight would escalate if the husband said – "It is my money. I will do what I like with it."

An **Ulterior Transactionis** one where one says something but means something else. Sarcasm is often involved in these transactions. E.g., Wife to Husband while window shopping in a Mall (child to parent) – "What a lovely saree. Can I buy it?" Husband to wife – "What a brilliant idea." (Meaning-what a stupid idea.) These transactions hurt and are undesirable.

The term **"Strokes" refers**to giving some kind of signal to a person. It can be verbal or nonverbal. It may or may not involve physically touching. Strokes are a form of communication and an important tool in building interpersonal relations. We all need strokes or recognition. For example, if we wave at a person or say "good morning" and the other person does not respond, we feel bad. Sometimes you will find that a child walks into the drawing room when guests are present with a minor problem which could wait. This indicates that the child feels neglected or left out and is looking for a stroke or attention. We expect or get used to a certain level of attention or strokes. When we do not get it, we make an effort to get it. A neglected child often breaks things, cries or fights to get attention or strokes. A neglected wife may raise minor problems, make demands or start a fight to get the attention she wants.

Strokes are essentially of two types, positive or negative. A **positive strokeis** one which makes the recipient feel good; one which makes him feel he is OK (alright or acceptable). Statements like well done, well played; what a lovely saree you are wearing; the pudding is out of the world etc. make the person feel good are positive strokes. Positive strokes should be used whenever there is an opportunity. Positive strokes can be conditional or unconditional. A **conditional positive strokeis** one that is given when the person receiving it deserves it. It must be given. Otherwise, the person may get demotivated and stop trying. An **unconditional positive stroke**is one that is given when it is not deserved. In such cases it may be taken as a sarcastic remark and spoil relations. Unconditional positive strokes given to women may make them suspect ulterior motives. Unconditional positive strokes given to a child by parents or grandparents may spoil him.

Negative strokesare those that make the recipients feel unhappy, inadequate and **Not OK**. These can be verbal and nonverbal. Not returning greetings, not replying to letters or missed calls, passing uncomplimentary remarks or criticism are negative strokes. Negative strokes can be conditional or unconditional. A rebuke for a mistake, poor performance in studies or at the workplace constitute **conditional negative strokes**. These can have a positive effect on the recipient and motivate them to put in more effort. However, **criticism must be in polite language and not abusive or nagging**. Abusive negative strokes or nagging may actually demotivate the recipient and cause resentment. Unfair criticism or rebuke constitute **unconditional negative strokes**. These are demotivating, will produce unhappiness and severe resentment. Among equals, this could lead to conflict or break up relations and trauma.

Strokes are an essential part of our lives. The kind of strokes we get and give leave a deep impression on our psyche and personality. They determine our life positions. We must ensure that we give conditional strokes whenever possible. We must try to give positive strokes whenever we can to our children, spouses, friends and colleagues.

The term **life position** describes our perception of ourselves in relation to people around us. There are four life positions. The first is **"I am not OK- You are OK"**. This is the life position in which we are born. As a child we are weak and dependent on our parents. All the elders seem stronger, more capable and more confident. Adults in this life position suffer from an inferiority complex. They are unsure, diffident, a receding and quiet personality who does not express opinions and speaks only when spoken to. A new bride at her in-laws place, a college fresher or a young person at his or her first workplace could be in this state. Some in this life position could be disadvantaged in some way. It may be their financial state, caste, lack of intelligence or education or physical prowess. They are shy; avoid crowds and parties. They may be very talented in their field of specialization and need to be encouraged to give their best. They can be very loyal and supportive of those who appreciate them. This life position is reinforced by negative strokes. This life position is reinforced when a child or person is repeatedly told that he or she is useless or when others are shown more affection or appreciation as the person starts believing that he or she is actually incapable or inadequate. Most women in India are in this life position because of the preference for a male child, restrictions on their movement and personality development and economic dependence. Persons in this life position make adequate subordinates but poor leaders.

The next life position is **"I am not OK-You are not OK"**. This life position develops when a person is neglected, maltreated or constantly humiliated. Women harassed for dowry in a hostile environment and without support of parents, weak children bullied in a class or workers tormented by their superiors are often in this state. These people think poorly of themselves and the world. They live in a world of despair. **They can be in a depression and may even commit suicide unless given psychological support**. Persons in this life position do not make good followers or leaders. They need to be given positive strokes or encouragement to get them out of this life position.

"I am OK-You are not OK" is a life position that develops in a child who is the only child or child of rich and powerful people who get unconditional positive strokes. **People in this ego state are arrogant and suffer from a superiority complex.**Many of them have a neglected childhood which makes them think "you are not ok." Most of them are rich, powerful, successful in professional life or of high caste or birth. They are authoritarian and bullies and are always trying to make people feel inferior. They have scant regards for others. They are not appreciated but tolerated. They have few friends and many "hangers on" who try to take advantage of him.

"I am OK-You are OK" is a life position that develops when children develop into successful persons under the guidance of nurturing parents and a positive environment. These persons develop competence and confidence without losing support of their parents, relatives and friends. **When a person is in this state, he is happy with what he is and happy with the world**. These people are confident but friendly. They are easy to deal with. They make great leaders and are also good subordinates and life partners.

Life positions of a person is the result of the experience gained by a person as he or she grows up at home, in a new environment or workplace. **Life positions are not permanent.**They can change as a person progresses in life based on their successes and failures and the encouragements; they get from people around them. Treating newcomers into the family or organization with respect, affection and guidance about their role and ensuring adequate positive strokes will reinforce the child's or newcomer's faith in people and the organization. They will gain confidence and reach the life position I am OK- You are OK.

Studying transactional analysis helps us to understand why people behave the way they do. It helps us to learn to communicate more effectively and avoid conflict.

Non verbal communication can be of many types. We have **written communication.** Written communication is precise, semi-permanent and can be stored and read over and over again.

These days with mobile video, even verbal statements can be recorded and preserved. They can then be sent or circulated on **social media**. We also have e mails, messaging and chats. These are modes of modern-day **digital communication**. Grandpa does not use social media as he considers it meaningless timewaster and a threat to mental and physical health. Over exposure to mobile phone is bad for eyes. He recommends that digital communications, particularly social media should be used with care to avoid its misuse or adiction.

Then we have **gestures, tone and body language**. Gestures and tone emphasise verbal communication by adding emotions to what is said. Body language can reinforce or contradict verbal communication. We must control our gestures, tone and body language to avoid conflict. We can use gestures, tone and body language to emphasise emotions during verbal communications.

Signals and sign languagewere an important form of communication before the advent of wireless and mobile phones. American Indian used smoke signals to communicate with nearby villages. Bugles, drums and other musical instruments are also used to pass information or mobilise people.

Silencecan be a form of communication. Silence has to be evaluated in the context of the silence. Silence in reply to a query normally indicates inability to answer. It may also convey contempt.

Successful leaders and managers mustunderstand verbal and non-verbal communication. They must **learn to communicate effectively**.

We must learn to communicate with people without creating conflict. Some simple rules given below will help reduce conflict.

Do not sermonize when someone is seeking sympathy. When a child falls, the mother does not blame the child but the floor. The best path is to avoid sermonizing all together.

Cold logic does not work with emotional people. If one cannot share the sentiments, a silent exit on some pretext may be the next best option.

Don't be a spoil sport when people are partying or having fun. You can always withdraw on some pretext.

Do not try to impose your will on others. Agreeing to disagree is a good method of ending an argument and avoiding conflict. I have told a friend of mine that if he valued our friendship, politics is a topic we must avoid.

Some **dos and don'ts for effective communications**are given below.

We must learn to listen. Communication is a two-way process. If you do not listen carefully, communication will not be effective.

Mind your tone. Unpalatable things if said in a proper tone are more acceptable than when said in anger, or apathy. Avoid sarcasm. Sarcasm is not wit. It invites resentment and conflict.

Mind your body language. Body language should match what you say. People are not dumb. Body language is more truthful than words.

Do not criticize others. It is never helpful. It is alright to correct your children or subordinates, even your wife, parents or others when they do something wrong. But such counselling should be done in private. Do not criticize others when they are not present. This is a popular pastime but invariably leads to conflict.

Do not discuss things when you are angry. Avoid discussions till you have cooled down.

Do not go on repeating the same thing over and over again. That is nagging. Nagging is perhaps the most irritating and destructive form of communication.

Do not say, "I told you so". Past cannot be changed. Damage has already been done. Saying I told you so can only create antagonism.

Do not boast. If you are good or rich, others would certainly know about it. Humility helps in building relations.

There is an old saying, **"Keep your words soft and sweet.**You do not know when you may have to eat them".

Learning to communicate effectively is an essential step to managing life. The ability to communicate effectively is important for effective managers for three reasons: It enables us to explain to others what we want. It enables us to build relationships and make friends. It enables us to communicate without creating conflict.

We cannot build relationships or manage people without effective communications. We must learn to appreciate people. We must learn to wish people, to give a smile when we meet them and to ask about their welfare. (Positive strokes). We must learn the art of small talk, of talking about weather, sports events and avoid discussions on politics, religion and other controversial topics except with those who share your views or belong to the same party. We can ignore people or be rude to them at our own peril. One gentleman in Grandpa's colony either ignored his neighbours or was rude to them. He invited sixty people to the funeral feast of his wife. Only four turned up.

CHAPTER SEVEN

LEARN TO MOTIVATE PEOPLE

Anyone who needs the help of another to do what the person wants has to motivate people to enable them to achieve their goals in the short and long term. As manager, he or she has to get work done through others. As parents, they have to motivate their children to study; to learn values; to participate in household chores. As housewives, they have to get the maid and other staff to work sincerely and efficiently. As supervisors, men and women have to get work done by workmen working under them. Principals of schools and colleges have to get their teachers and professors to give their best. The list is large. Most of these people have not been to management schools. But they have to **motivate people**. In this chapter, Grandpa gives some tips on motivating people.

First let us try to understand **motivation**. We do some things as a reflex action without assigning any motive. Some examples could be eating, sleeping or watching TV. The same activities could also have some purpose or motive. For example, one could eat to gain weight, lose weight or to celebrate. We could watch TV to know the latest news, for entertainment or to broaden one's knowledge. **Motivation is a person's reason for doing an activity**.

Persons use motivators to motivate others or themselves. Grandpa is not going to go into the theories of motivation as taught in management schools. Neither does he intend to use management jargon. He will try to explain what are motivators and how **motivators**can be used to motivate others.

Fearis one of the oldest and most commonly used motivators. There are many kinds of fears.

Fear of dangerfrom predatory animals and enemies motivated prehistoric man to form tribes or groups who lived together, hunted together and fought together.

When Grandpa was in school, **fear of punishment**kept silence in the classroom. The moment the teacher left, there was bedlam in the class only for order to be restored when the next teacher came in. Fear of punishment is used to maintain discipline in schools, armed forces and other organizations.

Fear of failureto achieve desired goals motivates persons to work very hard and give their best.

Fear of rejectionmotivates persons to conform to group values or activities. Peer pressure is a form of fear of rejection. It makes people follow fashion trends, take to smoking, drinking and drugs. Peer pressure in the form of regimental spirit makes soldiers overcome personal fear and face enemy bullets and take up dangerous assignments. Fear of rejection makes lovers dress well, use perfumes and deodorants and spend more money than the person can afford.

Fear of hunger also motivates persons to leave the love, affection and security of their families and venture in search of a better life into an unknown world where many dangers like death, economic slavery or refugee camps lurk. Millions of Africans try to cross the Mediterranean Sea and try to reach Europe in dinghies every year in search of better life. Hundreds of thousands of people from Central America walk hundreds of miles through mountains and jungles, ford rivers, brave dangers from robbers and mafia to reach the US. In India, millions from rural India head to the large cities in search of work and often live in inhuman conditions in slums and labour camps to escape hunger.

Fear of deathor Injury motivates some more than others. It can motivateus to take vaccination and avoid risky activities like driving fast. It motivates us to wear a helmet when going on a two-wheeler or working at a construction site.

Desireis another basic motivator. Like fear, desire also has different connotations. **Desire to please**is a very common desire. Children try to please their parents and teachers. Spouses try to please each other. Employees work to please their bosses. Government servants try to please their political bosses.

Desire for wealthis a very common motivator. Many join government services, particularly police, revenue services, income tax department, customs for the bribes that come their way. Many cheat on taxes. Many work honestly for long hours and neglect their family and their health. Many make risky investments and become millionaires. Many lose their all. Many take to crime to get rich quickly.

Desire for poweris also a motivator. It motivates people to join politics, administrative services and police. It leads to bitter rivalries among peers for promotions in the corporate world.

Desire for acceptanceshould not be confused with desire to please. Desire to please is directed to people in positions of authority. Desire for acceptance is more oriented to a group or team or even society or subordinates. It is a desire for gaining popularity; to be called "he is a jolly good fellow" or he is a nice guy; a helpful person. This desire prompts us to be nice to people, help persons in need and treat all with due respect.

Desire to servehas motivated many to give up a comfortable life to serve the people of a country, or disadvantaged sections of the society. Netaji Subhash Chandra Bose resigned from the Imperial Civil Service to lead India's armed struggle for independence. Mahatma Gandhi left lucrative and prestigious practice as a barrister in South Africa to lead fight against apartheid in South Africa and later lead India's non-violent struggle for independence. There are many lesser mortals who have given up promising careers to run orphanages and NGOs for benefit of the disadvantaged in societies.

Desire for gloryis what motivates sportsmen, singers, dancers, artists, models, actors to put in enormous amounts of hard work and undergo a lot of physical and mental hardship to compete and excel in their chosen fields. As and when they reach the top, money begins to flow in. But the real motivation is a desire to win or to excel.

Desire to achievetheir goals without desire for rewards also motivates some persons. In management jargon, this is called "**self-actualization**". This form of motivation can be seen in teachers, social workers, researchers, writers etc.

Financial rewardsare also motivators. This is used by sellers to lure customers with prizes, discounts, and cashback. High interests, doubling money in a short time are used by crooks to cheat gullible and greedy investors.

Self-esteemcan be a motivator. It motivates special forces, spies, persons engaged in rescue missions to take up hazardous missions. It makes people reputed to be honest to keep their word or financial commitments. It makes people behave in a dignified way.

To be a successful manager, a person has to master theart of using motivators. The same motivator does not work on all persons. An efficient manager selects motivators depending on the person to be motivated and the situation. Fear is most effective against small children and people who are illiterate or less literate. Desire can be used to motivate ourselves to study hard, do professional courses and to try to earn more money. Rewards like incentive linked bonuses and promotions are used in organizations to motivate their staff.

Setting a personal exampleis a very important motivator. Examples set by parents encourage their children to take part in household activities and behave in a dignified manner. Bosses, officers of the armed forces, teachers all need to set good examples for their followers.

Using positive strokesis another way of motivating people. **Praising good work**, particularly in front of others, motivates almost all to greater efforts. Praising a well-cooked dish will encourage whoever cooked it to greater efforts. **Accepting failure**where a person has tried his or her best also motivates the person to keep trying.

One must also understand **demotivators** and avoid using them. Demotivators are actions on our part that discourage people from giving their best. Some common demotivators are **unwarranted or unfair criticism, public rebuke**which destroys self-esteem of the person rebuked and **nagging**. **Ignoring**people and their work can also demotivate them.

Lastly, one must understand the difference between compliance and commitment. **Compliance**is acting or behaving as directed. It is motivated by fear or reward. The person stops acting or behaving as directed as soon as the motivation disappears. Thus, students start talking in class when the teacher is not there. Superseded employees will rarely work hard. **Commitment**is the willingness to go all out to achieve the objective. Committed persons are ready to make sacrifices to achieve the goal. Commitment comes from loyalty to a leader or person and belief in the cause. **Loyalty has to be earned through leadership qualities.**This aspect is dealt with in the chapter on leadership.

CHAPTER EIGHT

MANAGING PERSONAL FINANCES

Grandpa is a novice at managing personal finances. He had no money to manage till he retired. He and his wife specialized in making their money go as far as possible. They travelled with a kitchen trunk in the luggage boot of their two door Standard Herald with their children, stopping under a tree and cooking meals. On their first trip to Goa, they drove in their car, stayed in a dormitory, cooked breakfast and lunch in the parking lot and had a whale of a time bathing in the sea, drinking beer and going sightseeing. Grandma cooked, stitched clothes for herself and her children. She also worked as a primary school teacher, executive house keeper in a hotel and took tuitions. Their daughter boosted her pocket money by taking tuitions and satisfied her desire for fashionable clothes by buying dresses from "Fashion Street" and footpath vendors of Colaba in Mumbai. Grandpa and Grandma somehow managed to get their children educated and settled. With financial loan from his daughter and son in law, Grandpa even has a grand house. He gets a good pension and does not have to manage his finances. **So, be careful and do not learn wrong lessons from this narrative.**

Grandpa got Rs 4 lakhs from his provident fund account when he retired from the army in 1991. He thought he was an intelligent person and would be able to make money on the stock market. He invested half the money in shares. It got wiped out in the Harshad Mehta Scam of 1994. He has thereafter put whatever little money he had saved in the **PublicProvident Fund**(PPF). He finds PPF to be a very handy and perhaps the best investment for those who do not know much about investing and have no money to lose. It is the only investment Grandpa has. That is because

PPF gives almost 8% interest and the **interest is tax free**as of date and cumulative. It is deposited with the State Bank of India and is **100% safe.** There is no compulsion as to how much to deposit. **To keep the account active**, we must deposit at least Rs 500 per year. The maximum one can deposit in a year as of date is Rs 1.5 lakhs. The deposit can be made at any time in the financial year. Once the account is in operation for five years, it is **the most liquid fund**. One can withdraw half the balance in the account in 15 mins. The account has to be **extended after 15 years**for 5 years at a time. The account can be transferred from one city to another. However, it is best to have it at the town of your permanent residence.

One of his friends gave Grandpa **some tips on planning investments**. He does not vouch for their correctness. However, he is going to share them with his readers. They can use them after checking their soundness with a knowledgeable person.

To find out the number of years required to **double your money at a given rate**, just divide 72 by the interest rate. Thus, if you are getting 6% interest, you will require 12 years to double your money. Grandpa is not sure whether this doubling is before or after deduction of tax. **The value of money is constantly going down.** When Grandpa joined the army in 1963, his first salary was Rs 450 PM. When his daughter joined Citibank in 1989, her first salary was Rs 5000. His grandson, who joined an IT company in 2021, will probably get a first salary of Rs 60,000. It will be seen that **fixed deposits are not a great idea unless your income is non-taxable.** However, an amount equal to one year's expenditure should be in fixed deposit. This is to cater for the contingency of job or earning loss for any reason whatsoever.

To see how long it will take your **money to get reduced by half due to inflation**, divide 70 by the rate of inflation. Thus, if the inflation rate is 4%, your money in fixed deposit will be reduced to half its value in 70/4 or 17.5 years.

Corpus required to stop workingis 25 times your annual expenses. Thus, if your annual expense is Rs 6 lakhs, the corpus you need to invest in a reliable pension fund is Rs 600,000x25=Rs 1.5 crores. Grandpa is not sure if taxes and inflation have been taken into account.

Try to **save at least 20%**of your income. No harm if you can save more.

Try to build an **emergency fund**to cater for situations like loss of job or losses due to natural calamities. The fund should be equal to at least one year's expenditure. Thus, if your monthly expenditure is Rs 50,000 you should aim to have an emergency fund of Rs 6 lakhs. This money should be in the form of bank fixed deposits so that they can be easily cashed when required.

Never go beyond 40% of your income as **EMI.** This Rule is generally used by Finance companies to provide loans. You can use it as a guide to avoid a debt trap. Buy by paying the full amount even if you have to cash a fixed deposit. It saves a lot of money; far more than what you would earn as interest.

Try to pay your credit card bills within the month they are raised. **Credit card companies charge a criminal interest of 3% per month or 36% per year**on the balance outstanding. **This is against 12 to 18% interest you pay on personal loans or pension loans from any bank.**Grandpa is not very sure about the economics of EMI for consumer durables as he has always paid in cash for consumer durable including cars he has bought. Those who love money may like to do an analysis the advantages and disadvantages of buying with a personal loan from a bank and EMI.

Each person should have a **life insurance policy**to provide security to his family in case of his untimely death due to any reason whatsoever. The question is what should be the amount assured. **Some say it should be 20 times one's Annual Income.**Grandpa does not agree. If you start a policy early, the premium is less. But at the time one's Annual Income is likely to be low. Let us say that you start your career at an Annual Income of Rs 6 lakhs. 20 time six lakhs is Rs 1.2 Crores. What will be the premium? Can one afford it? **Is buying a flat with a loan a better option than having a large insurance policy?**The sum assured should be decided after taking into account various factors like the family wealth and assets, wife's family wealth and assets, whether the wife is a professional or house wife, whether the wife is entitled to family pension. **Grandpa does not consider insurance to be a very profitable investment.**The sum assured should be worked out by each person after consulting parents. One can have another policy after marriage in consultation with the wife and an additional policy after the birth of each child.

Grandpa has not given any tips on **investing in Mutual Funds, Equity or Debt Funds**because he does not have any knowledge about them. However, he has studied the history of Dow Jones from 1920 to date. It used to crash periodically, the most devastating one was during the Great Depression. **The last major crash was in 2008**. After that crash, the US Fed and the European Central Bank have been buying hundreds of billion Dollars of toxic stocks every month and ensuring liquidity in the market. Mutual Funds in India have been able, through constant advertisement, to convince a large number of middle-class investors to invest in mutual funds using the **Systematic Investment Plan (SIP)**. This results in injection of about Rs 10,000 crores of liquidity every month in the Indian Stock market. This has ensured that there is no crash and values of stocks keep rising. Grandpa does not know how long this injection of liquidity can or will continue. Many investors say that **stock markets are in a bubble**which is getting bigger by the day. But **no one knows if or when it will burst**. Everyone is happy making money while the "sun" (sic}) stock market shines.

Grandpa is of the opinion that **there are two kinds of investment which are not eroded by inflation**but appreciate with time. These are **gold and real estate**. Gold was Rs 150 per 10 gm in 1966 when Grandpa got married. Today it is around Rs 45,000, a rise of about 300 times in 55 years. It had crossed Rs 50,000 a few months back. Some volatility can always be expected in any investment. It is liquid to the extent that most banks give loans against gold. **The main problem with gold is keeping it safe.**Bank and private or well-hidden home lockers are the best places to keep gold. Land prices and prices of flats also appreciate with time. Grandpa bought the plot of his house at Rs 150 per square yard in 1995. The price today is Rs 45000 per square yard, a rise of about 300 times in 26 years. Prices of flats also rise but not to the same extent as land. **The liquidity of real estate investment is poor.**It is difficult to find buyers when one needs to sell, particularly for expensive properties. Grandpa knows of many who have not been able to sell their properties since demonetization. The capital gains tax and registration fee are also high and must be taken into account when investing in properties. Grandpa is also against buying flats before the project has been completed. He says that **persons who are buying flats with hard earned money saved should only buy ready to move in flats even if the cost is more.**Grandpa has seen too many projects, even taken up by reputed builders like Unitec or J K Group stall for many years.

Grandpa would like to end this chapter on managing personal finances by saying that we are different by birth, by our personality, risk profile and circumstances. **We have to manage our finances our way**and not by following X or Y. Everyone should study the subject and make informed decisions.

CHAPTER NINE

BEING AFRAID IS GOOD

There is a saying in Hindi, "Jo dar gaya, woh mar gaya." It means that anyone who is afraid is dead. Grandpa thinks that the opposite is true. Anyone who is never afraid will soon die. **The fearless are dying all the time.**They over speed while driving their motorcycles, cars and trucks and are daily meeting with accidents. Hundreds of thousands die every year in these accidents and maybe five times the number are getting maimed. The fearless do not wear helmets when riding two wheelers and when working at worksites and have their heads cracked when there is an accident. Fearless devotees in thousands throng religious places without masks or social distancing in COVID 19 times and get infected. Some of them die. Fearless political leaders and their supporters do the same at political rallies with similar disregard for COVID 19 infections with similar results. Thousands of fearless people die around the world while taking selfies at dangerous places. Thousands of fearless young people die while swimming in unknown waters during picnics or excursions. All these deaths and the pain these deaths cause to relatives and friends could be avoided if these individuals knew fear and took reasonable precautions.

Grandpa was always risk averse. He was never afraid of the dark or ghosts. As a young man he trekked hills and forests alone. But he never drove a motorcycle in his life. He considered the motorcycle unstable and preferred the scooter though it was less macho. He rarely ever drove or allowed taxi drivers to drive at speeds over 80 km per hour. He always avoided swimming in unknown waters. He was disciplined and did not do a single punishment during his stay at IMA.

Grandpa could overcome fear when the need arose. Need arose many times during his tenure in the Army. He had to do and supervise live mine training and live grenade throwing. As a young officer, he had to do a few flood relief operations. When his regiment built a Bailey Pontoon Bridge across the River Beas for a military exercise, he sat on top of the first tank that crossed the bridge. Once, as Chief Engineer of a Border Roads Project, he was visiting the construction site of a hill road near Nasik. His move to the top was stopped near the top by the site engineer. An attempt at blasting had gone horribly wrong. Some of the charges had not gone off. Explosive filled holes with detonators and detonating cord could be seen in the pieces of rocks lying all over the place. The dozer operator was afraid to push the rocks with his dozer. There was no other way to clear the road. Grandpa sat on the dozer next to the dozer operator and asked him to slowly push the rocks over the hillside. His presence on the dozer gave the operator courage. Together, they cleared the road in about half an hour. By God's grace, none of the explosives went off. When Grandma had to go into isolation after contracting COVID 19, Grandpa joined her so that Grandma did not feel lonely. He spent fifteen days with her in isolation and boosted her morale. He took Zincovit, Paracetamol and Arsenic Alb as preventive and did not contract the disease.

Grandpa does not want anyone to be paralyzed by fear. But people need to be aware of dangers. **There is no need to take unnecessary risks**. The world would be a much safer place if drivers did not go over speed; if people did not drive after drinks; if people wore masks, washed hands and avoided crowded places where COVID 19 is rampant. Girls are less likely to be assaulted if they do not venture out by themselves at night and they avoid going to secluded places with their boyfriends where they can be cornered by gangs of tugs or even policemen and extorted or raped. Many motorists can avoid accidents or being robbed if they avoid travelling on highways late at night. Many drivers can avoid accidents if they acknowledge that they are falling asleep at the wheel and ask someone else to drive or take a tea break. If motorists have to travel at night due to some emergency, they should follow a bus or a group of trucks to avoid being stopped and robbed on the way. People would not lose money if they are not carried away by their greed and invest in unknown securities for quick profits or share bank details, credit card details or OTPs to get cashbacks, lotteries and so on. Ladies would not have their gold chains, ear rings snatched if they do not wear jewellery when they go for morning and evening walks. They could not have their mobile phones snatched while standing or walking on the road if they do not talk on the phone while walking on the road or at a public place like a park.

Grandpa thinks that the world is becoming a very dangerous place. With rampant unemployment and poverty and advertisements and movies and TV serials making a virtue of opulent living, all types of crimes are on the increase. He recommends taking care to avoid the following situations.

Parking disputes are dangerous. Many innocent persons have been shot or knifed during angry exchanges during parking disputes when the offender is an angry young man or a goon. A polite request with folded hands is more likely to bear fruit than angry abusive shouting.

Road rage can also be a killer. This is particularly so if the offending vehicle is a Bolero or a high-end SUV. These are favoured vehicles of antisocial gangs and VIP brats. Gentlemen and women will come to grief if they pick up fights with such people. Be patient and ignore them.

Young women need to be very careful while rejecting suitors. This also holds good for fights when in live in relationship where the woman wants to end the relationship. These situations often lead to the woman being murdered or having acid thrown at them. Rejecting suitors should be carefully planned and politely handled. The best way is perhaps to seek time to take parent's permission. Thereafter, the woman needs to go out of station for a period. If that is not possible, she needs to be extra careful when commuting. Wearing a helmet with visor, covering face with mask or a scarf, wearing sun glasses and wigs are options which should be considered. Breaking up a live-in relationship should also be very carefully planned. One way could be going to your hometown during festival season and then relocating.

Both men and women need to be very careful about online dating. Online dating will sooner or later lead to a meeting. It is here that the danger lies. Bold women wanting to lead an opulent life are snaring men, both married and unmarried and trying to establish physical relationships. Intimate moments are video recorded on mobile phones by accessories. Then either rape complaints are registered and out of court settlement reached on payment of a hefty sum or the person is simply blackmailed. The police act as mediators and take their cut. Alternately, there is black mailing by threats of posting videos on social media or sending photos to spouse or relatives. **The fearless have a lot to fear. Online chatting and**

sexual exchanges are also dangerous. These can be recorded and used for blackmailing for money or sex or both.

Giving lift has become very dangerous. One of my friends, while driving home alone from work, gave a lift to a young woman. When they reached a crowded junction, the woman told my friend that he should hand over all the cash in his purse. Otherwise, she would start shouting that he had molested her. My friend quietly parted with his money. Recently, two boys in an SUV returning from a tourist spot nearby gave a lift to a girl who flagged them and claimed that her boyfriend's motorcycle had run out of gas and she needed to get to a petrol pump. Once inside she demanded money. The boys refused to pay and the woman file a complaint of rape. When she refused to be medically examined, the police got suspicious. Soon the facts were out and the woman and her friend were arrested and charged with extortion. Giving lifts to men can also be dangerous. They may be armed and rob you.

Meeting in secluded places has become dangerous for coupleswhether married or otherwise. In a recent case in Mysore, the man was beaten up and robbed and the woman gangraped by half a dozen men. These kinds of incidents are quite common and many go unreported. Even policemen are known to extort money from such couples. Grandpa says that it is much safer to meet in crowded places like malls or markets. The safest place to meet is the girl's home.

Government jobs are the most difficult to find in India. Politicians often take money for giving jobs. A chief minister of a state spent years in jail after being convicted of a recruitment scam. **Many unscrupulous men take advantage of the situation to cheat desperate young men and women seeking jobs.**They pose as being close to the powers that be and demand large sums of money upfront for giving jobs. Only a few of those who have paid get jobs. Some lucky unsuccessful candidates get back the money paid in instalments. Most lose the money. Grandpa is against this practice. But who is he to tell anyone what to do? All he can say is that if a person has made up his mind to pay, he should make sure that the person is real and can be held if he fails to deliver.

Online fraud is the latest threat. It started about 20 years back with people getting mail saying that they had won a lottery worth millions of dollars in a foreign country. The mailer would ask for personal information like date of birth and mobile number and bank details for depositing the money. Once these details were provided, all money in the account was cleaned out. Now we have a variety of reasons for asking these details; renewing KYC, receiving cashback, and receiving matured life insurance details. Grandpa once received mail from a person who posed as a philanthropist wanting to donate to charities asking for the same details. Luckily, he didn't. But if you provide the details, your money will be gone. If you share OTP, your money will be gone. A person paid Rs 10 online to a charity and lost all his money.

The other latest threat is **online gambling**. Advertised by popular icons like Mahender Singh Dhoni, Virat Kohli, Saurav Ganguli and a number of sports commentators, online gambling sites like Dream 11, My Dream Eleven, MPL, etc. are encouraging young men and women to gamble online. Warning like there is an element of financial risk; can be addictive; play responsibly; are piously bandied. But the fearless young men and women are not averse to risks. But the end result can be tragic. Recently, a young man in Assam murdered his aunt when she refused to lend him her mobile phone to play these on-line gambling games. **Karnataka Government has banned on line gambling.**However, the Central Government has not.

The smartphone which is indispensable to many is also dangerous. Social media is prone to misuse and is often used for trolling, blackmailing and extortion. On line pornography is responsible for most of sex related crimes. Use of digital payment apps lead to online frauds. Watching movies and sports events on its small screen is damaging to one's eyesight.

Grandpa is fearful of slippery bathroom floors.A smooth tile or granite floor when coated with soap and water becomes very slippery. Many an aged people including his father have broken their hip bones in a fall in the bathroom. He himself had a fall in the bathroom but escaped with minor injuries. He recommends using skid-proof rubber mats under the shower and use of a plastic stool or chair to sit on and bathe with water from a bucket.

Grandpa says, "**Do not be fearless. Be risk averse. Learn to conquer fear**when the situation demands. Take all possible precautions when doing things. Do not covet what you have not earned. In doing so, you could end up losing your all."

CHAPTER TEN

Staying Healthy

Staying healthy is a challenge faced by most of us. The environment we live in is totally against staying healthy. The air quality in most cities is poor. Quality of water is poor in many places. The use of RO removes many essential minerals from drinking water. Many of the food stuff including milk, cottage cheese and spices we buy are adulterated, often with cancerous chemicals. Hormones are injected into animals and vegetables to make them grow larger and faster to enhance profits. Cancerous pesticides are sprayed on most vegetables and fruits to keep pests away. Apples and some other fruits are coated with wax so that they stay fresh longer. Acids are used to clean root vegetables like potatoes and ginger. Formaldehyde is used to preserve meats and fish. Then there is the temptation of delicious fast foods which are usually bad for health.

Stress, the prime killer, is our constant companion. Competition starts in the kindergarten and continues to the grave. We are always trying to meet the expectations of others; children are trying to meet expectations of parents; workers expectations of bosses; husband and boyfriends of expectations of wives and girlfriends and vice versa. The ambitious amongst us are working day and night to achieve lofty goals. Then there are problems with lifestyle. Long working or study hours leave little time to spend with family or to exercise. Many of us spend long hours on the computer and mobile phone which is bad for the eyes and back. Stress often leads to drinking and eating disorders which are bad for health. Men, as young as 30 are dying from heart attacks.

Grandpa has listed above some of the problems which we face in trying to stay healthy. But he is not trying to tell you what to do. He is not a doctor, dietician or psychologist. Who is he to tell you what to do? **Grandpa's USP is that he is a reasonably healthy 80 years old.**His hair is intact, he has not had a cataract operation or any prostrate problem. His teeth are gone and he had a stent placed in his heart in 2007. Both were possibly due to smoking which he started in 1962 and stopped in 2007. In this chapter, he is sharing his research and personal experiences in trying to remain healthy. He starts with tips on **eating healthy**.

The table below gives what our body needs and where to find it.

Name	Natural Source	Daily Dose	Max / day
Vitamin A (Retinol)	Cheese, oily fish, milk products, liver (max 75g /week), eggs, oily fish (sardines, mackerel), fortified low fat spread, carrots, sweet potatoes, broccoli, orange or yellow fruits and vegetables which contain beta carotene like carrots.	.7mg m .6mg w	1.5mg
Vitamin B1 Thiamine	Ham, soya milk, water melon	1mg m .8mg w	
Vitamin B2 Riboflavin	Milk, yogurt, cheese	1.3mg m 1.1mg w	40mg
Vitamin B3 Niacin	Meat, poultry, fish, mushrooms, potatoes	16.5mg m 13.2mg w	500mg
Vitamin B6 Pyridoxin e	Meat, fish, poultry, pulses, soya products & banana	1.4mg m 1.2mg w	10mg
Vitamin B7	Eggs, soya products & fish		0.9mg

Biotin			
VitaminB 12	Meat, fish, poultry	1.5mcg	2mg
Vitamin C	Citrus fruits, green vegetables	500mg	1000 mg
Vitamin D	Sunlight exposure most important, milk products, cereals & fatty fish	40mcg	100mcg
Vitamin E	Vegetable oils, nuts	4mg m 3mg w	540mg
Vitamin K	Cabbage, eggs, milk, spinach, broccoli, cucumber, cauliflower	1mcg/kg	1mg
Minerals			
Boron	Chickpeas, almonds, beans, bananas, walnuts, avocado, broccoli, apples & raisins		
Calcium	Yogurt, cheese, leafy veg		
Chloride	Salt		
Magnesiu m	Spinach, pumpkin seeds, curd, almonds & dark chocolate		
Potassium	Meat, shrimp, milk, fruit and pulses.		
Sodium	Salt, soya sauce		
Chromium	Meat, poultry, fish, nuts & cheese		

Fluoride	Fish, tea		
Iodine	Iodized salt, sea food		
Iron	Red meat, eggs, apples, banana, green vegetables, boiled raw banana		
Magnesiu m	Nuts, dates and tea		
Selenium	Organ meat, sea food, walnut		
Zinc	Spinach, pumpkin seeds, curd, almonds, prawns & dark chocolate		

Vitamins A, D, E and K are fat soluble. Some fat in the form of butter or vegetable oils is essential for the body to absorb these vitamins. Hence, we have the Western custom of using salad oil and the Indian custom of taking mustard oil with boiled vegetables, eggs and pulses. Some form of fat has been used in recipes since ancient times.

It is important to know the symptoms and reasons for **vitamin D deficiency**. The main symptoms are whole body/muscle pains and feeling tired most of the time; frequent infections due to weakened immune system. **The primary reason for Vitamin D deficiency is inadequate exposure of the body to the sun.** Avoid going into the sun from 10 AM to 4 PM. UV rays are highest during this time. If you are able to expose part of your body to the sun for 30 minutes a day before 10 AM or after 4 PM, you will not have vitamin D deficiency. Diet alone cannot meet your need for Vitamin D. Sun exposure or Vitamin-D supplements are necessary. Food rich in phytates like whole grains, nuts, seeds and legumes and oxalates which are plenty in dark green leafy vegetables deplete Vitamin D in the body. Eating too much leafy vegetables and whole grains is not good for those who have Vitamin D deficiency, particularly ladies. Vitamin D needs some other vitamins and minerals to work. These are Magnesium, Vitamin K, Zinc, Boron and Vitamin A. If you are deficient in Vitamin D, you should ensure you take enough of the above vitamins in your food or as supplements. Vitamin D is also essential for absorption of calcium by the body. Vitamin D Levels are very important for all Diabetics. Vitamin D deficiency leads to decrease of insulin secretion by up to 48%. Vitamin D directly acts on insulin producing cells in the pancreas to produce more insulin. Vitamin D reduces inflammation which is commonly present in patients with Insulin Resistance Syndrome and Type 2 diabetes.

Let us now know about **vitamins and minerals which are good for the eyes.** Ten foods which are a must for healthy eyes are fish (particularly **those rich in Omega 3 acids**like sardines, mackerel and other oily fish), nuts rich in Omega 3 Acids like walnut, cashew nuts, pea nuts, pulses, seeds (chia, flax, hemp), citrus fruit, leafy greens (spinach, methi etc), carrots, sweet potatoes and eggs (**Lutein and Zeaxanthin**). One needs to include more **glutathione**and antioxidant-rich foods in one's daily diet. Glutathione rich fruits are grapefruit, strawberries, and avocados. Also, eat food rich in Lutein and Zeaxanthin like corn, greens, eggs, and turnip greens. These may help prevent both macular degeneration and cataract.

Symptoms of retinal problemsare a sudden increase of **"Floaters"**. Floaters are the unusual spots in your vision. They may appear like black or grey particles scattered all over the place, or like strings and cobwebs intertwined. When the number of floaters seems to grow suddenly or exponentially, you should grow concerned. Other symptoms are:

- Sudden and annoying flashes of light that tend to make you feel uncomfortable.
- Tunnel vision is another symptom. Peripheral vision is either blurred or hazed. At times, it could be due to Glaucoma. However, it is also one of the signs of retinal detachment.
- Deteriorating vision or seeing a swaying black or grey curtain. Distorted images are clearly manifestations of a possible damaged retina. Injury in the eye may also cause retinal detachment.

Diet for persons suffering from cataractshould include a daily intake of Vitamin A 5,000 I. U., N-acetyl-cysteine 250 mg, Vitamin C 1000 mg, Vitamin E 800 I.U., Beta Carotene 25,000 I.U. Chromium 200 mcg. Zinc 15 mg. Rutina 250 mg. Quercetin Bioflavonoid 300 mg. Vitamin B-2 (Riboflavin HCL) 50 mg. Each person should formulate a diet out of the options available and take vitamin tablets or dietary supplements to get most of the needs.

Vitamin Ais a powerful antioxidant known to help maintain healthy vision and skin. It is responsible for producing the pigmented layer of the retina that aids the light-sensing rods and cones of the latter to carry on with their functions.

Carotenoidsare nutrients that make fruits and vegetables appear red, yellow, and orange. Carotenoids are found in the retina. Studies have shown that eating food with these nutrients lessen the chances of age-related macular degeneration (AMD) and cataracts. Food rich in carotenoids include eggs, broccoli, spinach, tomatoes, and zucchini. Omega-3 Fatty Acids are essential fats found in the eyes and brain.

N-acetyl-cysteine, a stable amino acid, has been shown to raise the levels of Glutathione. Cysteine is found in protein rich eggs. **Completely avoiding eggs may rob the body of this amino acid**which may have anti cataract properties. Eggs can increase cholesterol. However, cholesterol levels can be controlled by medicine. No other food is as effective in keeping our eyes healthy. Persons in teens should take two eggs a day. Old people must take an egg a day.

The lens of the human eye is bathed in a **vitamin** Crich aqueous solution which is 30 times more concentrated than the human blood. It appears that this vitamin C acts as an ultraviolet filter preventing the harmful effects of ultraviolet light. With age the levels of vitamin C begin to decrease and this may contribute to the formation of the senile cataract. There are several studies which have shown that high doses of vitamin C (1000 mg/ day) will reverse the development of some cataracts. High levels of Glutathione keep the human lens clear and prevent the development of cataracts. In one study, 81 percent of patients with cataracts were deficient in riboflavin.

Foods that produce **uric acid**should be avoided by those who suffer from **Arthritis and Gout**. These include red meat, organ meat, fatty poultry, bacon, fruit juices, aerated soft drinks and alcohol. Vitamin C reduces levels of uric acid. Do not give up on lean meats, fish, sea foods and alcohol. Reduce the quantity and frequency of these foods.

Some form of exercise is a must. Walking for half an hour a day five to six days a week is recommended by most doctors. "Pranayam" (a form of Yoga) is a very desirable form of Yogic breathing exercise which is very beneficial. Grandpa has practised it since 2007 when he had a stent inserted in his heart. But one should not overdo exercise. Grandpa recommends that the aged should enjoy exercising and not do what is tiring.

Management of Stress is essential for staying healthy. Stress can be avoided by controlling expectations, temper and ambitions, developing an attitude of gratitude and remembering "we win some and lose some." One should take failures and setbacks in their stride. One should never brood over the past because the past can never be changed. All we can do is learn lessons from the past. It is also ensured by living the life of a law-abiding citizen, avoiding greed and jealousy. Stress can be reduced by physical exercise, praying, listening to music, being with friends and family and doing things we enjoy. Any attempt to reduce stress by eating or drinking will be disastrous.

Good and adequate sleep is essential for good health. Seven to eight hours of sleep is required to stay healthy. However, many working in the corporate world, particularly in the IT sector find it impossible to get adequate sleep. Those working night shifts must get used to sleeping by day. Students must avoid studying late into the night or very early in the morning. The aged often tend to wake up very early in the morning. They must make up by sleeping in the afternoon or mid-morning to stay healthy.

Watching TV late into the night is a bad habit and will have an effect on one's health. Inadequate sleep can result in temporary loss of memory and weakness. It can also result in increased stress, migraine and even heart problems. Extreme sleep deprivation is form of torture used for interrogation of prisoners and terrorists.

One should try to **prevent cancerous (cancer causing) substances from entering our body**. Avoid smoking, chewing tobacco, water stored in black PVC water tanks or old disposable plastic bottles. Grandpa recommends peeling all fruits and vegetables which can be peeled including soaking and peeling almonds to avoid insecticides and pesticides. He tries to buy freshly slaughtered meat and poultry and wash fish and greens very well in running water.

Early detection of medical problems is essential for certainty of cure. You are the only one who will know if you have a problem. Grandpa says, "Do not neglect minor problems or they will become major." Grandpa tests blood pressure once a month. He is non diabetic. He does lipid profile; liver function and serum creatinine (for kidney function) test every four months. Grandma is diabetic. She does fasting and PP sugar test once a month, HBA1C once every 3 months and lipid profile, liver function and serum creatinine tests every 4 months. You can consult your doctor about tests and their frequency.

Grandpa would like to share with you his**way**of staying healthy. He feels that it is difficult to calculate whether his diet has given him the vitamins and minerals he needs. So, he uses Becosules Performance multivitamin tablets. Grandma takes Nurokind Plus as advised by her doctor. They both take LycoRed capsules, a dietary supplement containing Lycopene, zinc and selenium which is supposed to be a good antioxidant and beneficial for prostrate daily. There are many options available to select from. Grandpa takes a number of meals as given below:

7 AM Tea and Biscuits

9 AM Breakfast: 5 almonds soaked overnight with peel removed, fruit, porridge/corn flakes/dalia (crushed wheat) with milk, two toasts with one egg/one slice cheese/tinned sardines/mackerel and butter/ margarine and a glass of milk.

11 AM Some fruit and juice.

1 PM Lunch: Rice, dal or one vegetable, fish or egg dish and curd or raita

4 PM Tea and Biscuits

7 PM Whiskey and snacks

9 PM Dinner: 2 to 3 chapatis, dal or a vegetable dish and a paneer, chicken or egg dish

Grandpa tries to avoid stress by accepting events as the will of God. He **never looks at the past with regret but to learn from mistakes and never looks at the future with fear but to plan for it.** He does not compare himself with others. Grandpa and Grandma have learnt to appreciate others. Grandpa prays once or twice every day. But he does not go to religious places or sermons.

For exercise, Grandpa does "Pranayam" almost every morning and goes up and down 150 to 200 steps every day. He goes for walks when in the mood. He gets half an hour's exposure to sun while gardening.

Grandpa uses Homeopathy to prevent diseases. However, some of his readers are violently allergic to Homeopathy. So, he is not going into the subject in this book. Anyone interested may get in touch with him about it.

There are different types of treatment. Baba Ramdev, yoga teacher; industrialist; political personality has set a cat among the pigeons with his tirade against Allopathy. What is the truth?

Allopathy, Homeopathy, Ayurveda and other forms of traditional medicine like Unani (Muslim), Acupuncture (Chinese) etc are in use and are relieving the suffering of millions of people every day. Allopathy is only about 300 years old. Human civilization is over 5000 years old. The human race has survived nearly 5000 years without allopathy. All forms of medicines have limitations and are not infallible.

It is not out of place for **Grandpa**to share his personal experiences. He **is not dogmatic and uses all forms of medicines.** He would like to share a few experiences. When he had bouts of breathlessness in 2007, he did not try Homeopathy. He went and got ECG done. ECG showed a heart problem. He went to a hospital and got a stent inserted. Grandpa does not go to alternate medicine for life threatening diseases involving vital organs.

In 1968, Grandma had a severe attack of Pharyngitis while at a small town in Assam. It was a problem which occurred every year. Grandpa took her to a Homeopath. He gave one small packet of medicine. It was dissolved in water and took over three nights. She was cured for life. In 1985, Grandma had a severe tennis elbow and could not even put on her clothes. Grandpa got her treated at the Command Hospital, Kolkata for a month. All kinds of physiotherapy were done. There was no improvement. Finally, on recommendation of a friend, they went to a traditional bone setter (Old world Orthopaedic specialist). He put some liquid on the elbow and tied a bandage. The process was repeated two more times with an interval of a week. After 3 weeks she was completely cured. In 1993, Grandpa's daughter had a severe attack of Jaundice while at Chennai. She went to a reputed Unani Jaundice specialist and was completely cured in a week. When Grandma was found COVID positive with moderated infection recently in Chennai, she went into isolation and was treated with Favi Flu and a few other medicines. Grandpa also went into isolation with her so that she was not in solitary confinement. He gave her some Homeopathy medicines and took the same along with paracetamol, vit C and Zinco vit. Grandpa lived 20 days with her in the room without even a mask without getting infected. None of them had any major symptoms. CRP and D-Dimer tests show both of us to be COVID free.

Grandpa treats headache with Disprin, cough with Kuka syrup (Ayurveda), stomach upset with Pudin Hara (Ayurveda), my wife's knee joint pain with Doctor Ortho, a message oil (Ayurveda) and occasionally paracetamol. He treated a bereaved lady and her son with Arnica to help them get over their grief and take the husband's body for funeral. He also gave her homeopathic medicines to stop her hallucinations with great success.

Grandpa is not asking anyone to change their philosophy. He is only trying to explain this. **Prevention is better than cure.**Grandpa tries to improve his immune system by eating a high protein healthy diet; doing "Pranayam" in the morning, eliminate stress with "It is for you to strive, it is for God to decide whether you succeed" Gita approach; exercise without stress and preventive use of Homeopathy and Ayurveda. Every form of medicine, Allopathy or Traditional, works well for some problems and has limitations. None are infallible. Otherwise, no one would die from illness.

Early detection and treatment can make all the difference between life and death. This requires clinical tests at prescribed intervals and listening to your body. Do not allow problems to aggravate by delaying treatment.

The acumen and dedication of the doctor and not his qualification makes a lot of difference. May God give you the wisdom to select the right one for your medical problem.

Life is full of contradictions.A cardiologist says do not take eggs. Eye specialist says to take an egg every day. Grandpa's friend had violent pain in his thigh. A scan showed an old injury. One specialist said to walk only with a walker. Another said exercise and strengthen your muscles. My friend exercises but avoids putting stress on the knees and hip. The middle path is the best path. Finally, it is your body and your life. You are the only one who knows what you feel. Do what you want but **do not neglect problems.**May God give you the wisdom to do the right thing.

CHAPTER ELEVEN

PLANNING FOR RETIREMENT/OLD AGE

Grandpa's readers may not be anywhere near retirement or old age. But this is his only opportunity to discuss this very important issue. Grandpa will not be around when they retire. It is never too early to plan for retirement or old age. **Retirement is applicable to those who are employed on a salary.**Their job may be with pension or without pension. **Self-employed people do not retire.**They grow old and may have to give up their professions.

The main problem with growing old is the loss**of our physical and mental prowess.** The rate of loss differs from person to person. But be sure that no one will remain fit and fine forever. They will require physical support in household chores, in personal hygiene and grooming, travelling, recreation and most importantly company, love and affection. This support can be provided by family members or by professionals. Joint families living in harmony are not seriously affected by this problem.

Planning for retirement and old age should be different. Retirement comes earlier. Children may not be earning or getting married. Money requirement is more. One can work after retirement. Retirement plan must include the following:

Financial planningis most important. Money becomes very important when it is in short supply. One must work out requirements very carefully and be on the plus side on the requirements of children like cost of professional education, marriage, pocket money etc., own requirements like building a house, buying a car, monthly expenses etc. If there is a pension, it may not be enough. Income and expenditure must be balanced and a plan must be made to cover shortfall if any.

Next question that needs to be answered is **whether to take up a fulltime job, do part time consultancy or start a business**or simply enjoy a retired life. If you have to work on another full time job or part time consultancy work, you may require some training and some help in getting jobs. You should keep in touch with colleagues who have retired and are holding influential positions in the private sector. Subordinates who are doing well can also help in getting by recommending you to their bosses.

One must be very careful about starting one's own**business.**Grandpa is dead against **partnership business**. One of his army colleagues went into partnership business with his brother-in-law. After fifteen years his brother-in-law had a house in Banjara Hills, Hyderabad and he was on the street. Another army officer Grandpa met, went into partnership business with a local businessman in Alwar. He lost his all, sold his house and disappeared. When Grandpa came to Alwar, he wanted to start a diary business. He met a director of Rajasthan Dairy. He asked Grandpa if I was ready to live at the farm. Grandpa replied in the negative. The director told Grandpa to forget the idea as the staff would steal milk and fodder and the business would fail. He knew a colonel who had lost all his money on dairy business. Grandpa gave up the idea and started looking for a job. However, another army friend succeeded in setting up his own business. He did a hotel management course just before retirement and worked as manager in a hotel for a couple of years. Then he found a financier and built and ran his own hotel. He was a success.

If you are not settling at your parent's place, **where to settle**is the next question to be answered. This is a vital decision. Very few will have the money to repeat the process. Set your **decision criteria**. Mine was a small town; a military cantonment town; inexpensive; within 150 km of a large city and international airport and connected by train and highway. Grandpa evaluated three towns, Dehradun, Alwar and Mhow and finally settled at Alwar. Alwar did not offer employment or top-class medical facilities. Grandpa went to work at Delhi, Sholapur, Mumbai, Goa, Ahmedabad and Gandhi Nagar and returned to Alwar after assignments. For major medical problems Grandpa and Grandma had to go to Delhi or Chennai. After all, one does not fall sick very often.

One has to build a **support system**to cope with old age. Grandpa built an annexe to house a family when building his house. It was used by Prabhu, his army "sewadar", till Prabhu moved into his own house. Now Grandpa has got another family to stay there as a part time security guard, gardener and handyman. He hopes to make him his driver. Nearby village provides domestic help. At some stage, Grandpa and Grandma will need **professional caregivers**. They have been well settled at one place for 25 years. They have a good circle of friends and well-wishers. The doctor and the dentist have been treating them for 20 years. They see no need to move. After one of them passes away, the other may have to move to an old age home with assisted living facility or move in with their daughter. Grandpa will start looking at options and start evaluating them in a few years.

One way of retiring early and enjoying life is to generate adequate **passive income.**Passive income is money that comes from investment, royalty or brokerage. One does not have to physically work to earn money. The following can be considered:

Investments in **fixed deposits or pension funds**give passive income. One needs to have lots of money to invest to get the required income. The return gets eroded by inflation over the years. But the investment is relatively safe. In this connection, please refer to the chapter on personal finances.

Buying property and **renting**them out is a good source of income. Two of my army friends made good money by renting out rooms on the first floor of their houses to students or young executives. Getting a tenant to vacate a rented property can pose problems. It is easier to get students and ordinary people to vacate rented premises. The Government is bringing a new tenancy act which will make life easier for the owner. Farm lands, ponds and orchards can also be rented out. Cars, two wheelers, furniture, refrigerators and other household goods can also be rented.

Royalty from books, photographs, income from patents are also passive income. Commission or share of sales commission in direct marketing is also passive income.

Preparing for old agemust include provision of a support system that includes provision of meals, housekeeping, transport, medical check-ups and treatment. **Social interaction**is very important for mental wellbeing. Some who are not in good health or in extreme old age may need 24x7 personal care attendants. These days there are companies which provide support for senior citizens living alone in their own homes. There are also **old age homes**which provide all kinds of support that are needed. One must collect information about them and have a plan ready. It is desirable that siblings, relatives or friends decide to co-locate at an old age home. It also helps if the old age home is located within easy driving distance of supportive children, relatives, grandchildren or their friends.

The motto of boy scouts is "Be prepared". **Grandpa says**that everyone should have the same motto. **We need to be prepared for all eventualities at all times including for old age.**

CHAPTER TWELVE

PROBLEM SOLVING

If you are alive, you must be having problems. They can be minor, like the TV is not working or the tap is leaking. They can be serious like not being able to decide on a career or not getting a job. It can be very serious like getting the "Pink Slip" or a family member falling seriously ill. Whatever be the nature or seriousness of the problem, we have to tackle and solve the problem. In this chapter Grandpa will give you some tips on tackling and solving problems.

The first step and most important step is **problem definition**. Let us take an example. Your TV has gone blank. How would you define the problem? Would you say that the TV needs repair? You could also say that the TV is not working. If you define the problem as TV needs repair, you have decided that the TV has to be repaired and not replaced. But if you define the problem as TV not working, you have two options before you; repair or replace.

The second step is to lay down the **decision criteria**. The decision criteria must be laid down in advance and ranked in the order of importance. Let us say you want to go from Alwar to Delhi. There are three options. You can go by train; you can go by bus or go by taxi. The decision criteria are economy, travel time, comfort and transport requirements in Delhi. If we rank order comfort as 1; transport at Delhi 2; time 3 and economy 4; the decision will be taxi. If we rank economy as 1; time as 2; comfort as 3 and transport at Delhi at 4; the decision will be AC train.

Coming back to the case of TV going blank, the decision criteria in this case could be economy or cost of repair versus cost of new, reliability of the TV, urgency of having a working TV. It would also be necessary to collect information about cost of repair, cost of new one, time required for repair, time required for purchase, life after repair versus life of new one.

The next step is to collect and compare the information obtained in the form of a table as given below.

Decision Criteria	Weightage New	Weightage Repair	Score New Purchase	Score Repair
Life of TV 3	3	1	3x3=9	3x1=3
Urgency 2	2	2	2x2=4	2x2=4
Cost 1	1	3	1x1=1	1x3=3
Total Score			14	10

With the above decision criteria, the decision is to purchase new. However, one can do a **sensitivity analysis.**If the decision criteria were cost 3, life 2 and urgency 1, the score for repair would be 3x3+2x2+1x1=14 and score for new would be 3x1+2x3+1x2=11, the decision should be to repair.

To put it simply, define the problem, decide on the decision criteria, collect information and then decide how to solve the problem. Procrastination will not help. It is likely to make the problem worse. When there is only one option like paying a courier, it is called a programmed**decision.** But one must generate options and evaluate them. Only then will you get good, meaningful solutions.

You will occasionally make bad decisions and suffer losses or inconvenience. Do not cry over it. Past can rarely be changed. Learn lessons and get on with life. The journey through life is long, very long. Most of the time there will be an opportunity to correct our mistakes.

Be decisive. Take problems by the horn and solve them without delay. Inability to take a reasoned decision when required can be fatal. A bad decision is better than no decision.

CHAPTER THIRTEEN

KITCHEN OF SINGLES AND WORKING COUPLES

For reasons best known to them, generations following Grandpa's are less inclined to marry. It may be that they are worried about losing their personal freedoms. In some cases, persons choose to remain unmarried after broken love affairs because they lose faith in the opposite sex. Grandpa's son is 50 and still unmarried. He is by no means an exception. Even where a person is not against marriage, he or she has to remain single till they can get married. During this time, they may have to live by themselves away from their families. Even if married, working couples have very little time to spend in the kitchen. Even where the wife is a devoted and loving housewife, the husband may have to stay alone for periods due to the working environment. Couples where one of them is in a frequently transferable job may have to stay separate for the sake of children's education, looking after ailing parents or family business. Grandpa also had to stay separated from Grandma for short periods and manage his own kitchen. **Grandpa is of the opinion that to be called an efficient manager, a person must be able to manage their kitchen efficiently.**For this they must have a smart kitchen.

Efficiency comes from being able to manage time. To get maximum out of time, one has to be able to perform multiple tasks at the same time. Being able to cook while doing other chores or office work requires a degree of automation in the kitchen. Grandpa suggests that **a smart kitchen**must be equipped with gadgets mentioned below.

The **refrigerator**is a very important part of the kitchen even if it is located in the dining room or anywhere else. It enables you to store cooked and uncooked vegetables, meats, fish, opened bottles of pickles, sauces, condiments, mayonnaise, cheese, pizza toppings, ice creams and so on. The fridge should be as big as you can afford and have space for.

The **microwave**is found in many kitchens. Most use it for warming food. Grandpa does not like the microwave. Microwaves use infrared or other electronic microwaves to warm and cook food. Grandpa suspects that infrared rays may be destroying the food value of food cooked or warmed in microwaves. Also, you usually can warm only one item at a time. One can warm two to three items at a time in a rice cooker.

Grandpa is very fond of the **air-fryer**. He uses it all the time to warm dry snacks and to fry potatoes, brinjal, Okra or Lady's-finger, salami and sausages. A recipe book comes with the air-fryer. Grandpa loves to experiment with the air-fryer. He has toasted bread and warmed burgers in the air-fryer by preheating the air fryer at 180 degrees for five minutes and then putting the toast or burger in the air fryer for a few minutes. He also uses the air fryer to thaw meat, poultry, sausages in the air-fryer by placing them in the air fryer and cooking for five minutes at 120 degrees. He makes excellent pizza in the air fryer and chicken and mutton kebabs. The best thing about the air fryer is that you do not have to switch it off when the dish is done.

The **rice cooker**is a must in a smart kitchen. Cooking rice is just one of hundreds of things that can be cooked or warmed on the rice cooker. Like the air-fryer, the rice cooker also switches off automatically and whatever is cooked or warmed in it stays warm till half an hour after power is switched off. A recipe book also comes with the rice cooker. Grandpa also uses the rice cooker to boil eggs, fish, sweet corn and vegetables. He also uses it to steam vegetables for sauteing or making Russian salad. Grandma also uses the rice cooker to cook chicken curry and chicken biriyani.

In most parts of India, milk has to be boiled before consumption. Boiling milk is no easy task. One has to be present while the milk is being boiled and watch what is happening with great attention. Milk when it comes to boil will rise and spill out of the container in a matter of seconds. **Milk boiler**is the solution. This gadget starts whistling when the milk starts to boil. So, you can do other chores while the milk is boiling and go and switch off the gas when the whistle blows. Hence, the milk boiler must be a part of a smart kitchen.

Gas stoveis an essential part of all kitchens. However, with cooking gas price touching Rs 1000 per 15 kg, it needs to be used sparsely only when essential. Grandma manages to make a cylinder last two to two and a half months by using the rice cooker and airfryer. This is a problem. A gas connection gets disconnected if a cylinder is not bought in two months. A commercial cylinder seems to be the answer.

Induction stoveis a new generation electric stove. Grandpa's son has this system in his kitchen in Singapore. It is not popular in India and could have maintenance problems due to lack of support in small towns. Grandpa recommends this as a backup for the gas stove.

Proper tools are essential for efficient operation. Proper minor kitchen equipment like knives, peelers, weighing machines, liquid measuring glasses, pressure cooker, non-stick frying pans, casserole, strainers etc. are integral parts of a smart kitchen.

A wide variety of **semi cooked foods**are available in the market. Grandpa recommends that smart people must know what is available wherever they stay and make use of them to save on time spent in the kitchen. However, Grandpa is against frequent use of instant noodles, cup soups, cup noodles and pasta as these have very little nutrition value. Excessive use of cheese can also lead to high levels of cholesterol.

Eating healthy must not be compromised. **Eating healthy**has been dealt with at length in the chapter on staying healthy. To put it simply, cooking healthy food means using less oils, butter and "ghee" or clarified butter, using plenty of vegetables and fruit and proteins in the form of fish, lean meat, eggs, lentils or "dal", cottage cheese and soya granules or Tofu. One needs to avoid deep fried stuff. However, occasional intake of some deep-fried food like "Pakodas", French Fries, burgers, "Samosa" or "Kachori" will do no harm. Some other innovations and recipes are discussed below. Letting your taste buds enjoy themselves once in a while will do your health no harm. Depriving yourself of your favourite dishes will increase your stress levels while having them will reduce your stress level. Many keep snacking to reduce mental stress and end up being obese. Having the right balance is the key.

Hung curdis a healthy alternative to mayonnaise. Mayonnaise is 90% vegetable oil and hence not a healthy food. Hung curd is easy to make. Put three to four tablespoons of curd in a tea strainer and place the strainer on a cup or steel "katori" and let the water in the curd drain out for two to three hours. Your hung curd is now ready. Grandpa uses hung curd for marinating meat or chicken, for making Russian Salad and for dips to go with French Fries or Potato Chips. To make the dip take two spoons of hung curd, one spoon of mayonnaise and add any flavour like mint, Pudina, tomato sauce etc. You can add a few spoons of cheese spread of different flavours.

Grandpa likes to make **Russian Salad**whenever dinner or lung is of soup, sandwich, burger, kebabs or roast meats. It has plenty of vegetables and fruits. Many recipes are available for Russian Salad on the web. Grandpa has his own flexible recipe. He takes two cups of hard vegetables like broccoli, cauliflower, beans, mushroom, baby corn, potato and carrot and cuts them into small pieces. He then steams them in the rice cooker. He adds soft vegetables like peas and bell peppers cut into the steamer after a while. Once the vegetables are steamed, he puts them into a bowl and allows the vegetables to cool. To the vegetables he adds one cup of vegetables like apple, pine apple, grapes. He adds some salt, fresh ground black pepper, a pinch or two of mustard powder and a tablespoon of fine ground sugar. Then he puts two tablespoons of hung curd, one tablespoon of mayonnaise into the bowl and stirs the vegetables and fruits till the vegetables and fruits are coated with the mix of hung curd and mayonnaise. If the mix looks dry, he adds a little milk or cream and stirs the mix. One can also add boiled eggs or fried sausage cut into small pieces. Russian Salad is ready. It is best served cool.

Grandpa has seen marriages break up over the bride being unwilling to cook. He has also seen tensions building up between young married working couples over sharing of household chores. Singles have to manage everything themselves. Hence smart singles and working couples need to learn enough about cooking to live happily. They must also have a smart kitchen.

CHAPTER FOURTEEN

Be a Rational Pessimist

Grandpa is not the Government of India that he has to project a rosy picture of the future. He thinks that the future is not rosy at all. In Grandpa's opinion, the world is in a very dangerous state. The dangers can be classified into heads like **global warming and climate change, pollution, pandemics, cybercrime, great power rivalries, internal conflicts, rise of Islamic Fundamentalist and economic collapse.**

Man has exploited and destroyed nature not only to satisfy his needs but also to satisfy his greed. **Global warming**is the result. Global warming is the result of about three hundred years of over exploitation of natural resources by the so-called "Developed World" who colonized the other world and exploited the natural resources of their colonies to get rich. Large scale deforestation including destruction of tropical rain forests was carried out to sell timber and to grow cash crops like sugarcane, soya, grapes, indigo and opium. Forests are also cleared to create open cast mines for coal, iron ore, bauxite and other minerals. Our energy hungry world is spewing tops of carbon dioxide and other damaging gasses into the atmosphere. Increased levels of carbon dioxide and other gases into the atmosphere has resulted in global warming. Arctic ice and glaciers are melting at a fast rate. Many places in the world are recording the highest temperatures ever. Global warming has resulted in rising sea levels and tides and increased frequency of hurricanes and cyclones which has been devastating coastal areas around the world. It is now common for months or years rain to fall in 24 hours leading to flooding of areas and cities which never had this problem. These floods and storms cause great damage to homes and habitat, crops, industries and infrastructure and devastate regions and economies.

Global warming is also resulting in prolonged droughts and forest fires throwing millions of people into great economic difficulty and forcing migrations. No country has been spared the effects of global warming. No country has been able to take effective steps to reduce carbon emission or stop deforestation. Lobbies of multinational corporations and their billionaire investors are just too strong.

Pollution is primarily of three types, **atmospheric pollution, pollution of water bodies**like the oceans, rivers and lakes and **pollution of soil and ground-water**. Four factors are the main causes of pollution. The largest is **industrial activity**. Almost every form of industrial activity causes pollution. Factories emit greenhouse gases and toxic effluents. These find their way into the atmosphere, water bodies and soil. Larger the industrial activity, the higher the level of pollution. The second major source of pollution are **motor vehicles**. The trillions of vehicles plying the road release large quantities of carbon and toxic gasses like sulfur dioxide into the atmosphere. The third source of pollution is our **modern agricultural practices**which use large quantities of chemical fertilizers and pesticides. A portion of these is not absorbed by the crops and finds their way into water bodies and soil. It is said that so much chemicals have been washed down the Mississippi River into the Gulf of Mexico that the sea along the coast line has become so toxic that marine life has almost disappeared. The last but not the least is the **colossal quantity of waste**the world produces every day. We have **nuclear waste**produced by nuclear power plants which many developed countries export to hapless third world countries have to accept. The next and greatly damaging is the vast quantity of **electronic waste**that the world produces. These contain **rare earth metals**which are extremely hazardous. And then we produce trillions of tons of **single use plastic**waste which are choking up drains, rivers, lakes and oceans. Poor air quality in megacities causes respiratory diseases. Polluted water gets into living things and our food chain and causes cancer and a variety of serious diseases. Grandpa is worried about the pollution related problems that the future generations have to cope with.

COVID 19, the latest pandemic needs no elaboration. It has been around for a year and a half and there are no indications as to when it will end and normal life will return. The pandemic has affected hundreds of millions, killed over three million around the world and pushed hundreds of millions into poverty. Untimely and sudden deaths of breadwinners have pushed many families into economic distress. Deaths of parents have orphaned thousands of children and possibly pushed many of them into child labor and sexual exploitation. Lockdowns and travel restrictions have resulted in unplanned separation of families and traumatic situations. Possibly a fallout of biological warfare launched by China to establish its hegemony on the world, it is certainly not the last pandemic that will devastate the world.

Cybercrime and cyberattacksare on the increase. Some like the attack on North-South Pipeline in the US was for ransom. Others like attacks on electricity grids, banks, and air lines are causing havoc. Many governments are pushing people to use digital currencies and payment systems without adequate safety systems. Cyber-attacks could cripple banking and other commercial systems leading to cash crunch. They could also cripple essential services and create chaos. Grandpa is afraid of digitization and virtual wealth. He believes in cash, gold, cheque and card payments. He considers net banking too dangerous and too complicated.

Great Power rivalries between the US and NATO and China and Russiain the South China Sea and Middle East could lead to catastrophic wars. China's belligerence has gone unchecked for many years. NATO expansion has pushed Russia to take up offensive defense. One mis-step in brinkmanship could result in World War III with horrendous economic consequences and misery for the whole world. Israel-Iran enmity could destabilize the Middle East. Grandpa knows that these problems are beyond our control. He believes that one should always hope for the best but be prepared for the worst. He tunes into news channels like BBC, Al Jazeera, WION and the internet to be aware of what is going on in the world. He also believes that being forewarned is being forearmed.

Internal conflictsarising out of ideological, ethnic or religious differences and fanned by great or regional powers have turned prosperous countries like Iraq, Syria, Libya, Venezuela into failed states. Even poor countries like Afghanistan, Yemen, Congo, Mali, Sudan have not been spared. These countries have produced over 10 million refugees who have migrated to neighbouring countries and affected their economies. With eating and other rights of Indian Muslim minorities which they enjoyed since independence being denied and encroached upon and ethnic conflict raising its ugly head in the north-east and Kashmir, how long can India remain free from serious escalation in internal conflicts? All states, towns and localities are not equally vulnerable to communal, ethnic or racial conflict. Grandpa recommends that if you are located in a vulnerable place, please try to relocate to a safer city or locality.

Islamic fundamentalismhas been on the rise around the world. Islamic State has been defeated in Iraq and Syria at great cost to those countries. **Islamic State**still thrives in Afghanistan and Western Africa. With the Taliban taking over Afghanistan, Islamic State is likely to get a boost from taking over unlimited stocks of military hardware left behind by the US in their hasty flight. The Taliban will also take over the drug trade. President Erdogan of Turkey has promised to declare Turkey a **constitutional monarchy and the Caliphate in 2023**. One does not know what effect it will have on the countries of the Middle East and around the world. Grandpa does not think that Islamic fundamentalism will ever gain popularity in India. Muslim women who have substantial freedoms and opportunities which are enjoyed by Hindu women will ensure that. Increased literacy and economic prosperity will keep Islamic fundamentalism away.

Economic collapsein India and many other countries like the UK, Brazil, South Africa etc. cannot be totally ruled out. A major war with China and Pakistan could result in funds being diverted to sustain the war effort. Any major conflict in the Middle East will severely impact availability of petroleum products in India. Even without a war, crude oil prices are at eight years high. Prices of petroleum products in India are at all-time highs. Gas prices rose over 25% in the UK in the first week of 2021. A war in the South China sea will result in severe disruption of imports of vital products, components and spares from China, South Korea, Japan, Taiwan and Vietnam. Even without a war, there is a severe power shortage in China, India and the UK. This could lead to the collapse of many large companies and the stock market. Air lines and the hospitality sector are already on the verge of collapse. Corporate loan defaults will mount. Ripple effect will be felt on banks and financial institutions. Millions of well-paid and ordinary jobs will be lost. Real estate and education related industries could also be in trouble. Floods and droughts resulting from global warming and Government policies could create food shortages. Only the super rich and the rural economy will survive. Grandpa would like his followers to save for the rainy day and always be prepared for any eventuality.

A rational pessimistis one who hopes for the best but is prepared for the worst. Grandpa's suggestions for preparing for the worst scenario are as under:

Prepare a survival plan. Assess your risk in relation to each of the threats listed above and study the option of relocating to a safer place during a crisis, a **retreat**. Metros and semi metros are likely to be worst affected.

Identify a small town or suburb with adequate facilities, particularly water. This retreat should be powered at least partly by solar power. The plan should include a way of the family getting together at the retreat if required.

Keep at least two months' requirement in **cash, medicines and dry rations**at home. In flood prone areas, cash, documents, medicines and rations should be kept in lofts or on the first floor. Also keep a week's requirement of **emergency rations**which can be eaten without cooking like beaten rice, dates, tinned and precooked food, fruits etc. One must keep adequate stock of drinking water. Fuel tanks must be kept more than half full. Spare cooking gas cylinder must be kept full. Adequate stocks candles, toilet paper and tissues and match boxes must be kept at home and at the retreat.

If disruption of fuel supply is going to be for a long duration, one may like to buy a battery-operated scooter, rickshaw or car and keep it at the retreat.

One need not do anything right now unless you live in one of the areas affected by cyclones, floods or water shortages. But have an **implementable contingency plan**ready. Be alert to signs of impending disasters and act in time. Those who are mentally ready with a plan will not be in soup.

CHAPTER FIFTEEN

TEN LESSONS FROM THE ARMY

Grandpa served in the Army for 28 years from 1963 to 1991. He cherishes the memories of those years. He also remembers many lessons he learnt from his seniors, juniors and courses he attended during his career in the Army. This book is perhaps the right place to share ten of these with his readers.

The first lesson he learnt at IMA was to "**keep one leg on the ground**". This represents the basic military tactics of fire and move. One part of the force takes up position to provide fire support to the other part which moves to engage the enemy. In civil life it means that **we should always be balanced**. We should not jump risking all by committing entire resources on a single project but take small calculated steps towards our goal.

The second lesson he learnt was to "**know your men.**" As a young officer, Grandpa was told that he had to know the men he commanded, their strengths, weaknesses, family problems etc. This knowledge became comradeship by playing games together, training together and enjoying together during "Barakhanas" or feasts held periodically. Knowing your subordinates in any organization is very important. **It enables leaders and managers to select the right person for a task.**

The third lesson he learnt was to **build "Regimental Spirit" or team spirit**. Fighting, constructing, running homes or businesses are team activities. Motivated groups of ordinary persons led by a competent leader can achieve outstanding results through teamwork. It is regimental spirit which enable soldiers to make supreme sacrifices in battle and achieve the impossible. Team spirit is built by knowing each other, respecting each other, working together, playing together and sharing pain and problems together. **Team spirit is equally important in corporations and organisations.**After retirement, Grandpa was the team leader of a team of consultants engaged in quality control of the World Bank Project for rehabilitation of earthquake damage caused by the Latur Earthquake of 1993. His team consisted of five senior engineers, ten senior visiting specialist consultants, twenty-one junior engineers and another twenty administrative staff. They had to manage the quality of construction, repair and rehabilitation of tens thousands of buildings spread over Latur, Osmanabad, Sholapur, Beed and Satara districts of Maharashtra over a period of three years. To strengthen his team, Grandpa held a meeting of all members of the team on the last Saturday of each month at a hotel. In the morning feedback was taken from the engineers, technical problems were discussed and training was imparted. Families joined for lunch hosted by the company and got to know each other. After lunch, administrative problems were discussed and sorted out. The consultancy was judged the best consultancy by Government of Maharashtra. More than ten of the junior engineers are now general managers and three are successfully running their business. The Team has its own social media group and stay in touch even after more than twenty years.

The fourth lesson was to **concentrate resources**at the point of decision. Army taught Grandpa to concentrate resources where result is desired. This also implied that too many things should not be attempted at the same time.

The fifth lesson was the **method of analysing and solving problems**. The process is known as **carrying out an appreciation**. A book can be written on the subject. Briefly, one starts with a review of the situation and the problem. This results in identifying the **aim or goal to be achieved.**Next, we identify the **Terms of Reference**. These are constraints on availability of resources namely men, material, machinery, money and time. Thereafter, we **study the factors**or various causes and conditions which could affect reaching the aim or goal. Next, we evolve at least two different methods or courses of achieving the goal. We study the advantages and disadvantages and adopt one method or course. Based on this we make an **outline plan.**

The sixth lesson was the **planning cycle**. The planning cycle in the Army starts with **the outline plan**including tentative resource allocation. This outline plan given to the subordinates who are going to execute the plan. They examine the proposal and plan in great detail and come for a **coordinating conference**. At the conference, the commander or manager discusses all aspects, objections, demand for extra resources with his subordinates. There after the commander or manager makes the **final plan and issues orders and instructions**. The commander or manager takes the final decision. This system ensures that all those in charge of executing the plan have been heard and are aware of the constraints under which they have to achieve the goal.

The seventh lesson was **battle procedure or simultaneous action at all levels**. Any force in the Army has an order group and a working group. The order group consists of the commander, his staff officer and subordinate commanders who are going to execute the plan. The working group consists of the troops and resources allotted to do the task or operation. Battle procedure ensures that elements of the workforce move towards the work site or operation area and deploy in anticipation of orders. It also ensures that resources do not remain idle.

The eighth lesson was to **train your command**for the task and their roles. Proper training is essential for proper and efficient execution of task. It is important that each member of the team is aware of his role and trained for it. Training of one's successor or second in command is a very essential part of this training. This ensures that work does not suffer if the commander or manager in charge falls sick or has to be away for any reason whatsoever. This is rarely done in corporate organisations as the boss is worried that he may lose his job to a junior.

The ninth lesson was to **create and maintain a reserve**. Army lays great stress on creation of reserves of resources to meet unforeseen eventualities. **Reserves when employed have to be recreated.**There must be provision made while planning projects for escalation of rates of inputs or for modification of designs. Unless this is done, projects may stall.

The tenth lesson was **do not reinforce failure**. Army taught Grandpa not to allot additional resources on a plan or project that had failed or was doomed due to any reason.**One should not repeat the dose till the patient dies.**One has to try a different method or change the aim or goal if it is not attainable.

CHAPTER SIXTEEN

A FEW REQUESTS

Persons who are reading this book, born to well to do tax paying parents would possibly belong to the upper crust or top three percent of our society. They are likely to be an only child or part of a small family. They are likely to be located at Metros, semi metros or large towns or abroad, studying or working in air-conditioned environments and addicted to social media. They may be thinking of themselves as global citizens. Very few would be thinking beyond the needs of self and family. Grandpa requests them to:

Please **Know your country;**its history, its geography, its diversity of cultures and languages, its art and crafts, its economic strengths and weaknesses. Unless you know your country, you will not understand the people at your workplace or your locality, the business environment and opportunities and effectively interact with the people or profit from the environment. You will also not understand what is happening and why. The virtual world is a world of illusions. **The real world is very different; very harsh; very demanding.**

Please spare a thought for **the disadvantaged majority**who are struggling to make both ends meet. Amazon and other e-commerce companies will give you discounts and cashbacks. But the profits they make go to make the rich richer. When Grandpa buys vegetables from a vendor or grocery from the local shop, he pays more. But the money puts food on the table of the hungry or a dress on a bare back. **Please patronize local markets to the extent possible.**

Please **Buy Indian brands**wherever possible. Chinese products may be cheaper. They are often of poor quality and could be made with forced labour of Tibetans and Uighurs. When you buy imported stuff, you are helping a foreign country. When you buy Chinese goods, you are strengthening our number one enemy. **When you buy a product made in**

India, you help generate employment in your own country and help the country's economy to grow.

Please **Pay your taxes honestly.**That is the least you can do for your country.

Our **patriotism**cannot be limited to cheering the Indian cricket or hockey team. As J F Kenedy, US President once told the American people, "Ask not what the country has done for you; ask what you have done for your country." Small things, planting a tree and nurturing it, paying fees of a poor child unable to pay his fees, feeding the hungry, contributing to NGOs working on disaster relief will go a long way to make this country a better place to live in. It will also ensure a better future for our children and grand children.

Please be **multidimensional**. We live in a globalized world; a fast-changing world and a dangerous world. We have to interact with people from all parts of our country and all over the world. They would be from different ethnic societies, different religions and cultures and have different value systems. You have to understand them to live in harmony with them. We have to understand climate change, we must understand technology, we must understand economics and politics. Only then will you be able to understand events in the world and anticipate problems.

Please do not be **dogmatic**. There is no such thing as black and white. There are only shades of grey. Look for logic or reason. Common-sense is the most valuable sense. Dogmas were created to control illiterate masses who were unable to think clearly or to reason. Dogmas are irrelevant in a world where ethics, morals, climate and technology are constantly changing. One must adapt to survive.

Please **Read a newspaper**, at least the headlines and be aware of what is happening in India and around the world. It will help you to forecast the coming events like travel disruptions, lock downs, supply chain disruptions and prepare to cope with the developing situations. Only local papers have local news.

Please **Do not be arrogant**. World's most powerful people, including Hitler and Donald Trump, could not control their destinies. No one can. **Seek God's blessings and protection.**Remember him and pray to Him at least once a day. Remember and thank your parents for bringing you up and helping you grow; your teachers and elders for teaching you what you did not know and all those who stood by you when you were in difficulty and made your day.

Please be careful with **your relationships. If you are married, nurture your marriage**. Just like a tree needs watering, marriages also need love or affection, mutual respect, positive strokes, sharing and caring. Ending marriages are painful in every way. An affair on part of your partner should never be the cause of parting. In many cases, one of the partners is responsible for pushing the other into an affair by neglect, nagging or own affair. Affairs pass. Draupadi lived happily with five husbands. Many Muslims live happily with four wives. I know two couples who were close to parting over affairs. They somehow stuck together and are happy in their end life. **If you are unmarried, be very careful in getting into relationships.**Physical attraction passes with time. It is affection, mutual respect, sharing and caring that are the bedrock of happy, lifetime marriages. In Rabindra Nath Tagore's novel "Shesher Kobita" ("The Last Poem"), the heroine has to choose between two suitors. One is rich, handsome, with brilliant wit and humour but moody and self-centred; the other middle class, average looking but extremely loving, caring, supportive and forgiving. She chooses the later saying, "I will garland the man who can make my life sunny even on a rainy day, one who will forgive my mistakes and still love me." **Breaking off relationships**is dangerous and need to be handled with great tact and finesse. Men are accused of rape; women are often attacked with knives or acids. Women need to be very very careful in rejecting offers of marriage or relationship from stalkers. Blunt rejection or abusive or threatening response can lead to reprisal attacks. It is better to say, "I am honoured, but need a little time think it over and consult parents." Then she must disappear from the scene for a time if possible.

Please **talk softly and politely**. More is likely to be achieved by talking sweetly and politely than by talking loudly and using abusive language. Using abusive language to reprimand angry young men is outright dangerous. Shouting should be an act of last resort when soft and polite talk is not heard.

Epilogue

Grandpa believes that **every person has an area he or she controls and a larger area that he or she influences. It is the duty of every person to improve what he controls and try to convince others to improve the environment.**Blaming others or the government for all that is wrong will change nothing. **We have to act to make our lives better to the extent we can.**

Grandpa believes that every person,man or woman, young or old, professional or house wife **is also a manager.Every person has to understand the basics of management.**Every person has to forecast what is likely to happen, decide what he or she has to do, make a plan, allocate resources and delegate responsibilities and execute the plan. Every person needs to have a contingency plan or Plan B to fall back upon if something goes wrong.

Grandpa is not Mr. Know All. But during his eighty years he has seen a lot, read a lot, heard a lot, experienced a lot and written a lot. **No one has to do what Grandpa suggests.**Grandpa chose his careers, his life partner, his lifestyle and his retreat. He was always clear as to what he wanted. He took input from many including his army "sewadar" before taking decisions. He analysed the inputs with an open mind and made decisions. By the grace of God, they have worked for him and he has no regrets. Grandpa expects his readers to do the same.

May God give everyone the wisdom to take the right decisions and grant them peace, prosperity and happiness.

Printed by Libri Plureos GmbH in Hamburg,
Germany